# Navigating Trans*+ and Complex Gender Identities

Also available from Bloomsbury

*Education and Gender*, edited by Debotri Dhar
*Gender, Identity and Educational Leadership*, Kay Fuller
*Sociology, Gender and Educational Aspirations*, Carol Fuller

# Navigating Trans*+ and Complex Gender Identities

Jamison Green, Rhea Ashley Hoskin,

Cris Mayo, and sj Miller

BLOOMSBURY ACADEMIC

LONDON • NEW YORK • OXFORD • NEW DELHI • SYDNEY

BLOOMSBURY ACADEMIC
Bloomsbury Publishing Plc
50 Bedford Square, London, WC1B 3DP, UK
1385 Broadway, New York, NY 10018, USA

BLOOMSBURY, BLOOMSBURY ACADEMIC and the Diana logo
are trademarks of Bloomsbury Publishing Plc

First published in Great Britain 2020

Copyright © Jamison Green, Rhea Ashley Hoskin, Cris Mayo, and sj Miller, 2020

Afterword © Meredith Talusan

Jamison Green, Rhea Ashley Hoskin, Cris Mayo, and sj Miller have
asserted their right under the Copyright, Designs and Patents Act, 1988,
to be identified as Authors of this work.

For legal purposes the Acknowledgments on p. xix constitute an
extension of this copyright page.

Cover design by www.ironicitalics.com
Cover image © h heyerlein / Unsplash

A catalogue record for this book is available from the British Library.

A catalog record for this book is available from the Library of Congress.

ISBN:    HB:    978-1-3500-6105-7
         PB:    978-1-3500-6104-0
       ePDF:    978-1-3500-6107-1
     eBook:    978-1-3500-6106-4

Typeset by Integra Software Services Pvt. Ltd.

To find out more about our authors and books visit www.bloomsbury.com
and sign up for our newsletters.

*Maybe you are searching among the branches, for what only appears in the roots.*
*~Rumi*

# Contents

# Contributors

**Jamison Green, PhD, MFA,** is an award-winning author and activist whose three+ decades of work to empower trans* and gender-diverse people and communities has had significant global impact. Dr. Green co-authored (with San Francisco, CA City Attorneys) the first city and county law in the US to establish civil protections on the basis of gender identity and expression. He later guided a six-year-long effort to remove prohibitions against transgender health from health insurance plans offered to San Francisco city and county employees and successfully leveraged that victory to national insurance reform equality in health care access. He was the first American transgender person elected President of the World Professional Association for Transgender Health, where his initiatives have increased access to medical education regarding trans*+ and nonbinary people globally. He is the author of *Becoming a Visible Man* and numerous articles in a wide variety of peer-reviewed, scholarly, and commercial publications.

**Rhea Ashley Hoskin, MA, PhD,** is a postdoctoral researcher whose work focuses on documenting and explicating anti-femininity (femmephobia) using her foundational work entitled "Femme Theory." Dr. Hoskin has received awards for inclusive research methods, and has been recognized as a Rising Scholar in the area of sexuality studies by the international Society for the Scientific Study of Sexuality, the oldest professional society dedicated to the advancement of knowledge about sexuality. Her work has been published in journals such as the *Journal of Social and Personal Relationships, Psychology & Sexuality, Atlantis: Critical Studies in Gender, Culture & Social Justice, Fat Studies: An Interdisciplinary Journal of Weight Studies,* and *Interalia: A Journal of Queer Studies.* Dr. Hoskin is passionate about using a wide variety of methodological approaches, ranging from popular culture analyses and theoretical interjections, to the physiological measurement of stress hormones in relation to prejudice and aggression.

**Cris Mayo** is Professor of Women's and Gender Studies and Director of the LGBTQ+ Center at West Virginia University. Publications in queer studies, gender and sexuality studies, and philosophy of education include three single-authored books, *Gay Straight Alliances and Associations Among Youth in Schools* (Palgrave, 2017), *LGBTQ Youth and Education: Policies and Practices* (Teachers College Press, 2013), *Disputing the Subject of Sex: Sexuality and Public School Controversies* (Rowman and Littlefield, 2004, 2007) as well as articles in *Educational Researcher*, *Teachers College Record*, *Educational Theory*, *Studies in Philosophy and Education*, *Policy Futures in Education*, *Review of Research in Education*, and *Sexuality Research and Social Policy*. Mayo is currently editing the *Oxford University Press Encyclopedia on Gender and Sexuality in Education* and co-editing, with Mollie Blackburn, a book on queer, trans, and intersectional pedagogies.

**sj Miller, PhD,** an Associate Professor of Teacher Education at Santa Fe Community College, is a trans*+ disciplinary-award-winning teacher/writer/activist/scholar, and an expert in secondary literacy across disciplines. sj's research is framed around trans*+ disciplinary perspectives on social justice, which cut across theory, epistemology, and pedagogy and link across socio-spatial justice. Currently, sj is Academic Studies Member of the LGBT Board for the National Council Teachers of English (NCTE); advisor for GLSEN's Educator Advisory Committee; co-editor of the book series, *Social Justice Across Contexts in Education* and Editor of the new series, *Spaces In-between: Beyond Binary Gender Identities and Sexualities*; column editor of "Beyond Binary Gender Identities" for the *English Journal*; advisory board member for Routledge's *Critical Studies in Gender and Sexuality in Education*, Palgrave MacMillan's *Queer Studies in Education*, the *Journal of Literacy Research*, *Journal of Adolescent and Adult Literacy*, *Teacher Education and Black Communities*, *Journal of LGBT Youth*, *The New Educator*, and *Taboo*; and UNESCO representative to develop *Education for Peace and Sustainable Development with the Mahathma Gandhi Institute*. sj has written eight books, over thirty-five book chapters, and over fifty articles, which have appeared in a number of journals including *English Education, English Journal, The Harvard Review, The International Journal of Transgenderism, Alan Review, Teacher Education and Practice, Scholar-Practitioner Quarterly, Journal of Curriculum Theorizing, Sex Education, Multicultural Perspectives, International Journal of Critical Pedagogy, the Educational Leadership Quarterly, Social Sciences, and Teachers College Record.* sj recently published the book *about Gender Identity Justice in Schools and Communities* and appeared in a feature documentary, Gender: The Space Between on CBS. sj presented a talk on gender identity justice for TEDMED, and is a contributor to the Huffington Post, BBC Radio, CBS News, and PBS. This past April of 2019, sj received the AERA Distinguished Contributions to Gender Equity in Education Research Award.

**Meredith Talusan** is an award-winning journalist and author of *Fairest: A Memoir* from Viking/Penguin Random House.

**Jessie Earl** is a filmmaker, pop culture critic, author, and YouTube personality. Her writing has appeared in Out, The Advocate, and Pride.com, among others. She has also helped to create several LGBTQ educational videos for The Advocate, which have garnered millions of views, as well as her on-going queer geek series *Nerd Out with Jessie Gender* for Pride.com. She has also done videos on shows such as *America's Funniest Home Videos* and spoken on panels for Los Angeles Comic Con, GLSEN, and The Advocate. She has also co-hosted several podcasts, including *The Advocates* podcast. She has directed several short films and won Tello Films 2018 "Pitch to Production" contest, earning her a production deal to create an upcoming transgender-focused sci-fi web series. She currently lives with her cat "Newt" in Seattle, working full-time as a content creator for Mighty Media Studios.

**Ashleigh Yule** is a school and child psychologist with a focus in LGBTQ+ issues, especially transgender health. She provides counselling, assessment, and consultation services for gender diverse children, adolescents, and their families. She also provides professional development and training for educators and clinicians to build competence and capacity in providing gender inclusive practices. She is a member of several transgender-focused organizations in Canada, including the Canadian Professional Association for Transgender Health, the Trans Equality Society of Alberta, and the Skipping Stone Foundation. She holds a Master's degree in School and Applied Child Psychology from McGill University and is a doctoral candidate in school and applied child psychology at the University of Calgary. Her dissertation research focuses on gender diversity in the autism spectrum. She is passionate about building capacity for gender affirming care for youth, families, schools, and community organizations.

# Preface

sj Miller

We are living in a time where understanding and recognizing the changes afoot about gender identity are becoming increasingly critical, err, vital. One might say we are in a gender re/evolution. While dangerous statistics offer insights about the harmful actual and attempted erasure and eradication of those whose gender identities threaten the comfortable and raise anxiety amongst cisgender folk, individuals are seeking support about how to lean into the process of being allies in the work.

Many people encounter others whose gender identities may differ from their own throughout their daily interactions whether at work, social gatherings, schools, in transit, shopping, and through observations in the media and social media outlets. When interfacing with others, they sometimes remain quiet in fear of offending someone, yet truly desire to understand, learn, and interact. So, how do we work through our own questions and concerns, and reach out to engage others whose gender identities can encourage our own growth? Where do we begin that conversation? Where do we begin that work?

This book takes up that call and is written to support the mainstream to become part of this re/evolution, but it isn't only written with those in mind. In fact, people with complex gender identities *also* want to know how to do the work and are seeking strategies to offer their networks. We (those of us with complex gender identities) hardly have all of the answers! This book offers support to cisgender and gender nonbinary people who seek to understand pragmatics and nuances of trans*⁺ and complex gender identities. It offers insights to develop and expand language and understanding about gender identities; strategies that can facilitate awareness (and diminish fear) about communicating with someone whose gender identity is complex and, in so doing, hopes to expand personal, social, and political awareness about gender-identity privileges in order for the reader to become an informed advocate.

The group that has come together to write this book, Cris, Jamison, Rhea, Jessie, Ashleigh, Meredith, and me, are deeply committed and vested in the efforts we each speak to in our respective chapters. The work moves from the political, into the landscape of gender identity shifts over time, the processes of communicating with others, cultural and media representations that both hold back and yet also advance gender identity critique, and how and what it means to be advocates in this work. Though our book stems from a similar place of concern that strives to create more equitable opportunities and outcomes for trans*⁺ people and those with complex gender identities, chapters in this work are complementary and can stand alone. Likewise, we approached research lenses, knowledge of the larger field about gender identity—which is limited in scope—and terms differently based on generational differences, viewpoints, life experience, and cultural, linguistic, bodily, and self-determined identities. As a team, we worked together, offering each other moral and educative support. We learned from and with each other as we deepened our own self-awareness. We are all on a continuum of learning.

Through the practical and exploratory strategies threaded across each chapter, this book takes readers on a journey that will advance awareness about how to understand, recognize, and develop nuanced language, how to confront and work through fears, and how to unpack communication patterns. It also provides resources for continued growth and support, and opportunities to reflect on the impact of these areas. This book supports both processes and suggestions for *leaning* into and *learning* about changes and shifts in gender identities by providing grounded, real-time, practical, yet research-based and solution-oriented ideas and language about how to be a better communicator, listener, and responder to trans*⁺ and complex gender identities.

As you develop your own toolkit, you are becoming part of the gender re/evolution, and everyone around you benefits. A hope for this work as you head into your daily lives is that gender identity becomes threaded across all aspects of livelihood: including but not limited to personal, educational, social, economic, cultural, linguistic, cisgender, professional, religious, medical, national origin and immigration status, religious and the political, and each trans*+-section of the indeterminacy of gender identity becomes part of ordinary existence.

We hope as you read, you will ask yourself questions, seek answers, and go out and live the work. We have much to do—and we can and will do it.

Your efforts are ushering in and galvanizing gender identity self-determination and justice. Your efforts are recreating a gentler and kinder world for those coming in.

# Foreword

Jamison Green

When I began struggling with the political and social ramifications of my own inability to conform to the gendered expectations of my assigned sex, it was the early 1960s. I had not heard of lesbians or gay men; I had not heard about Christine Jorgenson, America's first famous transsexual. I knew only that I did not fit into the "natural order" (as some might call the social structure in which I found myself). Others might describe my dilemma as rebellion against convention, but I did not dream of insurrection. I feared I was a disappointment to my parents and that I would never lead a normal life, have a family of my own, have a career, or even a job that would ever suit me. People told me I was a girl, but I could not be one. I didn't "think" or "believe" I was a boy; I did not hate my body; I felt left behind by all the promises of puberty that were being advertised to my classmates in the 7$^{th}$ and 8$^{th}$ grades. School was torture because I was required to wear clothing specified for girls, and I did wear a skirt, but I also wore crew socks and tennis shoes, an oxford shirt with a button-down collar, and a jacket that was as much like a baseball jacket as I could get my mystified parents to purchase for me.

I was lucky, in a way, that my parents were moderately indulgent of my stylistic choices. They valued reason, independent thinking, and childhood that was unencumbered by excessive rules beyond those required for physical safety. Sports and exercise were encouraged, though how those activities manifested was not forced upon either me or my younger brother. He, though, had no difficulties at all looking like what he was supposed to be. I, on the other hand, had a lower than typical voice, stronger than typical limbs, and excessive energy such that I was always moving, always busy, always planning something to occupy my mind and my body. My parents' indulgence would not last forever, but in the early 1960s I was still a child to them, not yet a young woman like so many of my school friends were desperate to become.

The politics of gender variance, or gender diversity, only became apparent to me almost two decades later, after I had been through six years of college and two degrees: BA and MFA in English. My parents imagined that I would become a teacher, but my intention was to be a writer. Writers didn't have to be a man or a woman; they could hide behind their characters and their words, and no one ever had to see them. I managed to find work as a writer within corporate settings, and I was able to get away with wearing slacks to work, and blazers, and the comfortable oxford shirts I loved. But by the late 1970s I knew there were people who changed their sex, who took cross-sex hormones, and had surgeries to make themselves more comfortable in their bodies so they could be more alive. I still didn't understand it all. My feeling about myself was that I was not transsexual (which was something I thought only male-bodied people experienced because they felt like women), but cross-gendered, which meant to me that "circuits" were "crossed" in my brain, making me look, sound, feel, and think more like a man than like a woman, but really I was something in-between, something not male and not female. And the best "solution" to my social problem was to transition to become a man, *a visible man*. Then I could stop worrying about whether others wondered about whether my body was male or female. I could just be myself, and people would think my body was male, and they would take me for granted, the way every other person who looked like what they felt like was able to be perceived, catalogued, and forgotten. I could then get on with my life.

By the late 1980s, there was a support group in San Francisco for FTMs, people who started life in female bodies, but moved into a male manifestation of themselves, whether that meant hormones or surgery or nothing more than clothing. In that FTM group, everyone was respected for who they were. Yet almost everyone was still afraid. There was no real "movement" then. There was an underground kind of world, and everyone worried about being discovered as if they were constantly living a lie. By the early 1990s, I said to my trans-identified friends I couldn't live that way any longer, and I thought no trans-identified person should have to live in shame and fear because of who they were.

Transwomen were already putting up some resistance. They didn't have the luxury of invisibility that transmen had. And some of them had put together organizations so they could help each other with housing, with meals, with finding work. But still there was no real movement, and almost no inter-group communication. People were geographically limited, economically and politically marginalized. By that time, I was in my mid-forties, and the thought of trans-identified people under twenty as having agency of their own was frightening. And yet we had already changed the world. We had already begun changing the language, raising consciousness about gender diversity, lobbying local politicians, participating on municipal committees concerned with human and civil rights, concerned with healthcare, police abuses. By 1996, I had appeared in three educational documentary films and contributed to the creation of two new laws. The internet was opening up new possibilities of communication, though it wouldn't be until 2000 that AOL, then the nation's largest internet service provider, would permit the use of the words "transgender" or "transsexual" in its public "meeting spaces."

By the late 1990s, high school students and younger were starting to identify themselves as transgender, and parents of young trans-identified kids were coming to meet me at the lectures I was giving across the country. They wanted to see if it was possible for their child to grow up to be a successful person, to get an education, to have a career, to live without shame or fear.

As the various authors of the chapters in this book will attest, there is still a lot to accomplish. Yet, there are some people proselytizing today who would have you believe that we have not accomplished anything yet, since there is still so much to do to provide equality and respect to trans*⁺ and nonbinary people in the US, let alone around the world. The authors here have much to say about where we are and how we arrived here; they have much to say about how to learn about who trans*⁺ and nonbinary people are; and, how to be effective allies in our efforts to achieve equal rights, appropriate healthcare, and social safety. But don't think for a minute that we haven't already come a long way, or that the young leaders of tomorrow are having to start from scratch. The important thing now is to make sure that the history and structures we've already built are not obscured or destroyed prematurely by the forces that oppose us, because tricking us into doubting ourselves, or into wasting time and resources by reinventing the wheel, is one of the easiest ways to keep us from making real progress.

Our emerging leaders are well-positioned to move us to the next level. Let's make sure they have the courage and the support they need to get the job done so we really can live in the kinder, gentler society we all deserve.

# Acknowledgments

We want to thank you, the reader, for desiring to make a difference in your lives; for the people you know, will come to know, and will never know. The gift you give is of yourself—knowing that you are part of a historic revolution and that the expansion of humanity as we know it will forever shift life on planet Earth. We hope that the work we invest in moves along a trajectory of *change*; one that *transforms, sustains,* and ultimately, *endures.* Though enduring will be far beyond the span of any of our lives, we cannot minimize the efforts of the work we undertake along the way. For the trails blazed, the paths made and walked down, the doors which are entered and exited, will collectively create a better world for those entering … and hopefully, for those exiting.

So, here's to you.
Here's to making a difference.
Here's to a kinder, gentler, and more just world.

# Transgender Generations and Technologies of Recognition

Cris Mayo

Several years ago, at a panel discussing gender diversities, a person in the audience asked if new technologies in gender transition would have changed the panelists' various, possibly generation-specific, responses to gender. It was both a good question and an indication that the ability to be recognized and embody gender are at least in part related to available technologies for such embodiment and recognition. Newer technologies seem to provide ways to be gendered that may be different from the possibilities afforded to previous generations. Access is still not certain or guaranteed and is reliant on access to insurance and health care. And even access to such technologies related to gender embodiment are not the full story of how generations respond to the possibilities offered. Thinking about the technologies of gender and the social formations of "generation," too, may provide a fuller understanding of how subjectivities unwind and connect across times, spaces, and their related possibilities. Questions like the one posed to the panelists can start us all thinking about the generational qualities to gender identities: what our genders might have been had we navigated social technologies of gender differently and what it means to now be living and working in communities of diversely arrayed senses of potentials for gendered subjectivity.

The generational technology/social formation/recognition constellation I will discuss in this chapter is not new. A 2017 editorial in *Scientific American* on the shifts in diagnosis, treatment, and legal recognition of trans people is also mindful of how science and social recognition complicate gender ("The New Science of Sex and Gender," 2017). The story includes a long passage on their magazine's warning, over 100 years ago, that the relatively newly accessible technology of the bicycle would be damaging to women's health ("The New Science of Sex and Gender," 2017). The potential for bodily damage was not the only concern; so too was the inevitable problem of women getting too far from home and chaperones. Technologies and social formations have never been separate, and while the particular affordances of technology have provided new ways of reconfiguring gender, the problem of the limitations of the gender binary and its embodiments are not new. The fact of technological improvement in gender transition is not enough to ensure access and acceptance—federal erasure of trans experience so close on the heels of what seemed to be some social progress show that social formations are not only related to medical technologies, they are also related to how technologies shape and are shaped by social recognition. But even this formulation may keep technology and recognition too separate from one another. To go a step further, Lewis Mumford (1934) suggested that social formations are technologies themselves, providing the relationality and connection necessary for innovations and that innovations, without their necessary social supports, are insufficient. Tools, he argued, have gotten too much attention. Without understanding the social contexts and formations in which cooperation and respect are supported, we don't understand how gender identities can creatively emerge. But as we think about the emergences of gender across time and social formations, increasingly we are also looking for ways to connect across generations whose negotiation of gender has been embedded in different technologies of gender-recognition.

Like the big tent of gender diversities that holds trans together, generational differences and continuities provide a way to think through how trans communities engage with one another and even prepare one another for the next potential shift. Connecting generations and spaces of transitions can help us see how, too, thinking about transitions as a state of gender, rather than a fixed and finished approach to identity, may help alleviate misunderstandings about what coming to gender identity may mean. Thinking temporally about gender and about subjectivity and community interrupts the stalled and solid sense of gender. Thinking through the times and places for/of gender may help our cross-generational conversations and help us to think about how we live and grow within genders.

In this chapter, using the idea of trans social formations, I explore some of the continuities and discontinuities in trans generations, drawing on conversations with older and younger trans community members, each of whom has lived in social relationships and technologies in different ways. The starting point for this tentatively maintains transgender as a social formation that includes a broad span of gender diversities, often in robust conversation with one another (Stryker, 2008). That generosity of social connection is reflected in Leslie Feinberg's *Transgender Warriors* (1996) and *Transgender Liberation* (1992), both of which keep historical and political connections across historical and contemporary gender formations, pushing at how normative power has constrained people but how people have pushed against the particular economic and political constraints of their various times to form new approaches to gender. As Feinberg notes, the decision to pass as a different gender may enable one to have easier access to employment. In historical cases, it may be difficult to discern whether the strategy was purely material—possibly affectional or gender-identity-related decisions could have been bound up in decisions to pass and it may also have been more socially respectable to claim material motives (as opposed to sexual or gender-identity-related desires) once one was found out. But the material motive for passing as a gender not attributed to one at birth, even if not a complete explanation, had the effect of highlighting the material inequalities as the basis for gender. In other words, the tactic itself discloses economic and political factors as structuring conditions for the gender binary.

If there have been important reasons for attending to shared economic and political constraints in varieties of gender rebellion, that attention to the convergences of gendered and agendered diversities does not rule out material divergences and specificities. Trans people's lives also have the very different relationships to social institutions shaped by isolation from a sense of connected community, whether through geographical isolation, racism, and classism or other exclusionary formations. Trans lives converge with other/overlapping issues related to gender and embodiment such as the diminishing access to abortion and reproductive freedom for women and/or trans people. I use "and/or" here advisedly, not wanting to erase the difficulties that women face, that ciswomen in particular face with regard to misogynies in law and practice, nor to erase the challenges of transmisogynies, too (Serano, 2007). Institutional exclusions and hate may not be exactly the same across divergent gender identities, but those shared if varied forms of exclusion are exclusions designed to limit agency and membership. The particular literal technologies are different—access to transition-related medical care or technologies that enhance reproductive choice—but the social formation of antitrans/misogyny are in many ways linked.

Focusing on divergent but shared forms of exclusion, Spade (2006) suggests that trans politics would do better to focus on how those exclusions shape experience rather than to outline particular attachments to one concept of gender or forms of subjectivity. Those exclusions, even if they seem continuous, are also framed differently across time, space, and identity. Attention to such institutional exclusions may lead to greater attention to particular convergences or divergences within the relatively big tent of trans and intersecting social formations as well. Namaste (2009), for instance, has argued that some of what we might take to be transphobic violence, especially that against transwomen of color who do sex work, may be more closely related to race/class/profession than transphobia in particular. Even if trans identities do occupy a large tent, this does not mean all have the same location or even duration of shelter within it. Namaste's (2009) discussion of violence experienced by transwomen of color sex workers may also raise the challenges of generational understandings of gender, as trans people of color experience violence and harassment, and pushouts from schools and families.

## Geography and Social Technologies

Thinking about issues of generation means considering more fully how particular locations and social institutions shape trans lives. In some ways, geography is its own kind of generational distinction—in cities and/or blue states, progress on trans issues may seem, legally at least, decades ahead of where it is in more rural, conservative areas. For younger people, all fifty states have laws against bullying that should protect LGBTQ students in schools and increasingly too LGBTQ students and employees are finding Title IX or Title VII-related protection from discrimination (federal acts protecting gender-based rights in education and rights against discrimination, respectively). While there are locations that are respectful, the lack of such protections and the increased activities against them at the federal level show that even such spaces are potentially limited in their impact. As in all contexts and all issues, policies, ordinances, and laws may set out an ethical ideal or even a procedural route, but without adequate training, advocacy, and resources, they aren't put into practice. In this political climate, it isn't clear whether exclusionary actions will continue to have consequences or whether those consequences will be constrained to particular geographical locations. In Kenosha, Wisconsin, for instance, Ash Whitaker won an $800,000 settlement against administrators who would not respect his, his mother's, and his doctor's decision to have him socially transition to confirm his male identity. This should have included correct use of pronouns and use of gender-appropriate restrooms— Ash was recognized by peers as a boy, it was adults who continued to not do so. Significantly for the growing use of Title IX and Title VII in such cases, the district decided to not fund an appeal to the Supreme Court and chose to settle. The settlement only requires that the district recognize Ash and Ash's right to use the correct bathroom; it does not extend to any other trans person. Like that reached by Gavin Grimm that only allows him (that is, not any other trans people) to use gender-appropriate facilities in his former high school, this settlement may not have an impact beyond Ash's experience, or if it provides guidance on another case it may not extend beyond the state in which it was decided. Localizing rights not only to particular locations but even particular people means that anyone else may still face discrimination.

That specificity of space becomes, in some sense, a kind of time in which trans people live, seeing progress elsewhere but not sharing a geographical or near-temporal access to it. I live and work in West Virginia, a state that the Williams Institute (Herman, et al. 2017) characterizes as having one of the US's largest proportion of trans people aged 13–17. West Virginia also lacks state-level protections for trans and LGB youth because it does not stipulate gender identity and sexual orientation in its antibullying policies. In addition, West Virginia lacks nondiscrimination protections on the basis of gender identity and sexual orientation, nor does the hate crimes statue cover or monitor crimes related to antitrans violence and homophobia. While eleven West Virginia municipalities have successfully added gender identity and sexual orientation to ordinances, and hopefully another is on the way shortly, navigating the patchwork of protections can be challenging for people of any age. Many people in West Virginia don't live in cities and ordinances do not cover those living out in the counties.

Despite the shortcomings in legal protections, the West Virginia state environment can be welcoming and there are longstanding trans and queer community formations and organizations working to make it even more welcoming. For instance, recently Fairness Parkersburg, an organization in the one remaining relatively large city in West Virginia that does not have a nondiscrimination ordinance that includes gender identity or sexual orientation, won the annual Christmas tree decorating contest. Their strategies to improve the lives of LGBTQ people who feel bruised from an unsuccessful campaign to make the municipal ordinance more inclusive have emphasized visibility and neighborliness. In the absence of rights, then, they have worked to change the community from within while also showing all generations of trans and queer people that they can be part of that space even if their rights aren't enumerated.

Despite these tactics that fill in for missing rights, there are significant indications to young people that the sense of belonging afforded to others in our small state are not afforded to them. While some area educational institutions like our flagship university, West Virginia University, have chosen to keep to Obama-era guidance on interpreting Title IX to protect trans students from discrimination, our state attorney general does not and he, like the governor, have signed onto an amicus brief to the Supreme Court asking that gender identity not be recognized as part of sex discrimination. Recent incidents underscore the sense of unwelcome. For instance, a sheriff's deputy at his second job as a school bus driver in Clay County, who—while in uniform and driving a school district bus—told a gay student, "No faggot activity will be permitted on this bus. In my Bible, it states that 'faggots will burn in Hell,' and I will not condone it." Trans high-school students have complained to their parents and friends that despite some lip service to inclusion, they are subject to harassment at their schools. Calls to administrators go unanswered. Gay-straight alliances have had their bulletin boards torn down. School personnel have shared that their Title IX officers don't know their responsibilities and, in some cases, don't even know they are Title IX officers. Calls to Title IX officers go unanswered. West Virginia's Big Brothers and Big Sisters organization won a grant to deliver training to help staff work with LGBTQ youth and as a result, lost $80K in donations and have had to end plans to extend their services to some West Virginia counties.

When trans people told a southern West Virginia activist collective, Queer Appalachia, that faith-based thrift stores and charities would not allow them access to clothing that matched their gender identity, Queer Appalachia started a coat drive. Like its work on harm reduction and addiction, Queer Appalachia uses grassroots, Marxist organizing to develop networks of care and support with queer community members in need. This year they have had requests for 7000 winter coats, accompanied by stories of the collision of racism, classism, and transphobia experienced by those requesting coats. The digital community that Queer Appalachia has created through their

Instagram presence and online zine, *Electric Dirt*, show the potential for reimagining space and community across spaces that may otherwise be isolated. They extend networks of support beyond geography that are nonetheless embedded in regional practices of craft and sharing.

While this kind of action can mitigate the sense of isolation, according to GLSEN, LGBT students in rural schools experience higher levels of harassment and abuse and neglect from teachers than do suburban or urban students (Kosciw et al, 2012). Further, rural LGBT students report a much lower rate of inclusion of LGBT-related lessons in schools than do suburban and urban students. Rural students were half as likely to have a gay-straight alliance in their schools (27 percent compared to 55 percent suburban and 53 percent urban). As I am in correspondence with a number of young gay and trans people (all of whom are in university) and in correspondence with some younger LGBTQ people in West Virginia, I'd also add the non-rocket science point that LGBTQ rural people can be very isolated. One young man's family found out he was gay but are now convinced that the intercession of their pastor means that he is not. They take his phone every night and have removed him from contact with his former friends. Another is also isolated at home with parents intent on keeping him there so he won't fall in with trans-supportive people. Deadnaming (using his birth name) and misgendering (referring to the gender attributed to him at birth) him add to his sense of isolation while at home but online connections to other friends and chosen family provide sustaining contact in the midst of that misrecognition. While these are only a few anecdotal indications of the challenges faced by LGBTQ students, they do map onto the usual challenges of rural trans and gay people: lack of social support, isolation from the LGBTQ community, and pressure from conservative religious people to convert to heterosexuality or remain in the gender assigned to them at birth.

Online resources help but access to computers or smart phones or even connection to internet continues to be a challenge for young people, especially those living at a remove from public libraries or in internet dead zones common in this mountainous state. The simple point may be that laws teach the broader population and that young people notice these lessons. In West Virginia, where laws, policies, interpretations of policies, and so on are still in conflict and in flux, trans youth are not unreasonably uncertain of whether they fit, whether they have options, or whether they can expect to be recognized and respected by peers and by adults and whether they have any recourse if they are trapped at home. Students hope that higher education offers them a way out but they also fear, like other LGBTQ students in many places, that if they are out as trans, they will lose parental support. Like members of other groups reliant on community support for their sense of identity, in this case regional identity, they fear that if someone from their hometown also attends the same university, their gender identity will be outed back home and home will no longer be home. Working with a graduate student trans woman on a trans training program, I asked how her hometown would respond to her transition. She preferred not to find out, expecting violence.

## Intergenerational Recognition and Struggle

More than a few of the young people who've contacted me or whom I have met do have wider networks for support—other people's parents, a caring teacher, or a strong family network. They know, or at least hope, that things are better for trans people in other places—even our LGBTQ+ Center's strongest donors are from out of state and have significantly bad memories of their time in West Virginia but remain committed to helping LGBT people who are still here.

LGBT adults have long argued that heterosexual-dominant communities are sending us LGBT young people who have no knowledge of their histories, their responsibilities to one another in terms of protection from HIV and STIs, and insufficient understanding of consent and responsibilities to partners of whatever sort of duration. The gaps in experience and sometimes access to healthcare between younger trans people and older generations need to be thought about carefully. As Riki Wilchins (2012) has observed, the older generation, especially those who transitioned post-puberty, have a different embodiment of trans identity than younger people who have access to hormone blockers or who identify as genderqueer, nonbinary, gender creative, and so on. Generationally non-continuous communities face these challenges (and arguably so do generationally sequential communities) in ways that may mean it takes extra effort to connect the generations into some form of not-necessarily-completely-cohesive social formation. Isolation in their born-families does not need to be their full story. Increasingly, where they can sustain connection on the web without parental interruption, younger generations are learning about their genders from virtual communities and popular media. Sense of connection across time and generation, one might hope, would supplement this sense of what is possible, especially in a time when trans presence is being intentionally erased from federal government websites.

Trans people are not the first to find protections rescinded and not the first group to be the focus of a concerted effort to remove them from view. Other communities can share information across their generations about their various struggles across time for recognition and their experiences of backlash. Generations of trans people, young and old, need spaces to work together and reflect on concerted efforts of erasure from federal websites and federal protections. It is worth having younger generations consider commonalities with other groups that have also fought for recognition and access to technologies and accommodations: lactation rooms, racially segregated restrooms and housing, redlining, and other forms of spatialized race, class, and gender divisions show that the struggles over restrooms are part of the territorialized struggles Spade (2006) discusses. Further, young people come to our communities without understanding the diversities of the people in them—they replicate the same racist, classist, sexist, and whatever else prevailing beliefs of their upbringing. They come to us bruised by homophobia and transphobia, and hurt by isolation, and while we all have some degree of experience working through the same challenges, honestly, we'd prefer they grew up with rights, with respectful recognition, and in communities that valued them, laws or not. And we might also prefer that they had connections with adults, if not as role models, at least as indicators that they will persist and flourish.

## Generational Gaps and Relations

Researchers have also examined how the family's generational understanding of gender potentially shapes how trans youth are positioned. Meadow (2018), for instance, in an analysis of the parents of trans youth notes that research attention to trans youth and increasingly "facilitative" parents are reshaping how transgender identity is defined in social relationships. For some trans youth, some transition processes may be confirmed by adults earlier but also potentially shaped by adult expectations for what gender should be, whether to protect their child from prejudice or protect themselves from social disapproval. Like Kessler's (1998) discussion of the gender normative pressures put on parents of intersex children, parents of trans youth have been encouraged by some doctors and counselors to make choices for their children based on concern about social stigma related to nonconforming gendered bodies and identities. Meadow, too, discusses the divergences in how parents and advocacy organizations for trans youth think of the problems related to gender. For some parents, children's trans identity leaves the gender binary in place, for others, young people are transitioning away from binary gender.

Such research on families may push against some theoretical analyses of queerness as interrupting reproductive time but it may also show the re-embrace of normativity within families with trans children. As Halberstam (2018) has pointed out, queer kinship is missing in the account of such families in Meadow's *Trans Kids*, a book much more focused on parents than kids (and with a fine explanation for that, too, although the title seems odd considering the necessary alteration of Meadow's research). The families Meadow interviewed largely keep to a narrative of protecting their children, whether from the problems of gender or the challenges of transphobia, and to a large extent, also attempt to protect some sense of normativity. By signaling their ability to notice "gender problems" and access medical care to solve them, families are both, of course, expressing care but also, in relationship with the clinical context of the children's transitions, moving toward greater "gender differentiation," not fluidity (p. 226). This study of families seems to indicate, if not clearly generational differences, at least differences between how those in parental roles think about their responsibilities and, potentially, how younger people are pushing against easy categorizations of gender.

Not all families of trans youth respond with re-normativizing narratives—the parents in Meadow's study, for instance, were associated with a clinic criticized for its gender-conservative practices to the point that it closed. Nor are the concerns of the parents about the safety and flourishing of their children unwarranted. Older generations are reasonably protective of the younger, but when such protections stall the possibilities of the younger generation, there is reason to be concerned about adult projections and anxieties (Farley, 2018). Determining when and how protections verge into problematic concretized identities has been a key challenge for thinking about how to educate queer youth without normalizing or homonormativizing them (Airton, 2013). Trans people do challenge gender binaries or upset what some might take to be embodied limits to gender and, arguably, removing that critique and just expanding gender may risk something like transnormativization. Trans people under this relatively new-seeming normative system, a continuation of gender normativity by other means, are only acceptable to the extent that they reinforce binary gender by living binary gendered lives. But increasingly younger trans people are also pushing against attempts to renormativize them.

If spaces and times for gender creativity are expanding, we have reason to be hopeful about the younger generation's ability to be creative and oppose gender norms. A very smart group of undergraduates led a discussion in one of my queer theories classes, which explored how various responses to the stipulations for gender dysphoria in the handbook used to provide guidance in medical and psychological diagnosis, the Diagnostic and Statistical Manual 5, might be answered by differently gendered classmates. Classmates identified with and against gradations of gendered dissatisfaction following no particular pattern of gender identity that would have been recognized by the document. Self-identified cisgender women articulated dissatisfactions that matched some of the categories; trans and nonbinary people disidentified with diagnostic markers. When discussion turned to medicalized forms of recognition and rights, ciswomen and trans/nonbinary people found commonalities in inaccessible healthcare and reproductive rights, but agreed that they had overlapping and divergent challenges related to embodiment and public space. The challenges to living in any gendered body are apparent in many states, but West Virginia has just had a popular referendum that removed abortion rights from the state constitution in preparation for the end of Roe v. Wade, the 1973 Supreme Court decision that linked the right to privacy with the right to make reproductive choices, nationally. The parallel between trans people seeking medical care in the state, which is not as accessible as it might be, and ciswomen seeking to ensure access to reproductive freedom with the one abortion provider remaining in West Virginia, may provide this generation with a way to understand the need for coalition work. Susan Stryker's (2008) *Transgender History* makes a similar case for the relationship among forms of gender transgression and forms of gender-related activism, keeping a firm connection to feminist activism while also understanding that particular sites of difficulty in navigating gender identity sometimes track alongside feminist issues and sometimes swerve. The transgender military ban, once again being pushed by the executive branch, and insurance companies and pharmacists working to deny women birth control, each highlight the difficulties of living in particular gendered bodies. Political formations, in other words, may be helping to create a sense of common struggle.

While some students argued that none of this would be in an issue if we lived in a genderless world, older trans people in town have been thinking and talking about how processes of getting gender markers changed on documents has changed in the last several years. To some extent, then, at least in this small community, younger people are aiming at hopeful and expansive definitions and the older generation is more focused on more immediately pragmatic issues of how to be recognized for who they are. Last year when undergraduates organized a student group for trans and nonbinary students, publicity about that group was shared with another trans group in the area that was mostly comprised of people older than undergraduates.

An older community member later described lingering outside the door of the meeting room, hearing vocabulary that didn't match her experience. She was concerned her approach to being trans would not be recognized by the students, who seemed to have an academic sense of expertise in gender studies that seemed to negatively judge her life. The group's critique of normative gender seemed to not invite in someone whose navigation of gender had to take into account employment and family ties. The students used specialized terminology that seemed to contain implicit critique of her hard-won sense of self in a social context that did not provide enough space for generalized demands for recognition. But her sense of their comfort at being out may have missed that they felt comfortable being out there, in that group and in that space but, as I'll explain shortly, not comfortable everywhere.

As more people in the community learn about the longer-standing group to which she belongs, younger people are starting to attend. She finds the generations are interested in one another and they, too, come with different vocabularies and expectations for institutional recognition. For younger generations, living in their authentic gender, for instance, may be a greater concern than shifting between that self and also needing to pass in the gender in which their families and employers have known them. sj Miller (2019) has described the younger generation as creating "micro-sanctuaries" to protect themselves from transphobia in public schools and this sense of "micro-sanctuary" also nicely describes the sometimes private/public worlds that older trans people have made to open space for gender identity that does not yet have that space in family or work contexts. Keeping separate phone numbers and privatized email accounts, closely held locations for meetings, and other careful cautions may seem like generational divergences to younger trans people who are able to live openly. But those seemingly generational cautions are, perhaps, not that different from the shifts between being out in one context and unlabeled in the next.

In the space of gender studies classes and trans/nonbinary group meetings, students do seem to be largely able to be out to one another. They are not out in other spaces, not even several hundred feet away from their meetings or classes, a strategy that speaks as much about local climate as anything else. Their conversations about what being out means continues the longer conversations in trans and queer theory about the perpetual function of normative power to reconfirm and recognize one back into someone who conforms. They know, too, that even with reassurances that they have recourse to change their names on rosters or make official complaints about transphobia, they may have to interact with people along the way who are not supportive. They often don't feel they can afford the interaction. The difference in experience or vocabulary that might have been overheard from outside the door of a meeting may look more like similarity when one of those group members inside the room is in a public setting instead of among friends. I'm saying nothing especially notable by saying that social formations that enable recognition, again like Miller's micro-sanctuaries, are contingent formations, reliant on time and space. The degree to which they are durable relies on the other social formations in which they are embedded or through which they must move.

The organizer of the very student group that the local trans woman listened to from the hallway, for instance, helped organize a very solemn event related to an intersecting identity-membership. They could not find welcoming space to articulate the connection they felt between being nonbinary and also being a member of that intersecting identity community, although they spoke very movingly of the resistance to hatred at the vigil. They felt forced to choose to represent only part of who they are and so hit the limitations of new forms of openness and vocabulary around gender. Their experience reminded them, too, of persistent exclusions from that intersecting group membership on the basis of gender and gender identity. Gender closets are everywhere and when coming out as nonbinary or trans means losing a sustaining space in another community, that trade-off is not so easy. Another student leader, a nonbinary person of color, shared a similar challenge with maintaining a space for their nonbinary identity outside of queer community using different names and pronouns when in different communities. Having been the person calling out names at a graduation ceremony, I admit to having been startled to see someone I knew as nonbinary with a nonbinary name, come up to get a diploma in a non-nonbinary gender presentation and a gender-specific name. Students have also shared that particular spaces on their various university campuses, not surprisingly if we think of social formations as localized, are spaces where they will revert to normative pronouns or forego identifying as trans or nonbinary. They do not think of these practices as analogous to the closet and that conversation is quite interesting. Miller is right that their assessment of space and relationality leads them to practices aimed at protection. They seek moments of recognition with friends that signal "don't out me," but also argue against an historical continuity with other forms of staying hidden.

Toby Beauchamp (2018) has suggested that as educators we need to be careful about being too critical of students' terminologies and strategies. Their terminology and, I'm suggesting, their strategies of social relationship, are navigated in spaces that "at times put pressure on 'transgender'; in many cases they are well aware that … rubrics fail to adequately address the nuances of their identities and sweep them into a formalized category that may well be at odds with their own identifications" (p. 26). Beauchamp suggests approaching technologies of recognition through "unanswerable questions [that] might generate new intellectual and political possibilities" (p. 28). We may find these unanswerable questions are approached by different generations slightly differently—or we may find that what is common among generations is having to think about those questions at all.

Among these new possibilities might also be an enhanced respect for older strategies, rethinking whether those seemingly outmoded strategies like the closet are a complete mismatch for new forms of safety-related complex navigation of times and spaces. A conversation among generations of trans and nonbinary people and allies led to an encounter that started with frustration at the inability of people to understand one another's struggles but ended with a concrete explanation of why navigating a relatively small, and as yet untouched by nondiscrimination policies, city was sometimes so challenging. Barbara, a trans woman who joined a recent workshop I was running, explained that she is only sometimes respected as a trans woman at work although she very clearly presents as female. She works at a restaurant chain that does not require name tags but has made her own to settle any question about her presentation and name. Three different managers work throughout the week. One recognizes who she is, and uses the name and pronoun appropriate to her gender identity and presentation. One initially recognized her name and pronouns but has since drifted into renaming her and using pronouns clearly at odds with her gender identity and presentation. The third utterly refuses to use a name other than her masculine birth name and masculine pronouns. Every month she copies the managers' schedules into her phone using a color-coded system: green for the manager who recognizes her, yellow for the manager who used to recognize her, red for the manager who does not recognize her. Every morning before going to work, her phone shows her what kind of day it is going to be: recognized, partially/maybe recognized, or actively disparaged. Her navigation of transphobia using new technologies was a striking indication of how much generations share and how pervasive barriers to recognition can be.

But Barbara also shared how, forty years earlier, her mother had supported her gender identity, encouraging her to pick out skirts to wear at home (while cautioning against doing so at school for fear she'd be bullied). Stories of such kindnesses may be, one hopes, another way for generations and kinship networks to grow. A young teenage trans man, brought to the university-sponsored conversation on trans issues by his mother, was in awe of Barbara's strength and asked if they could hug. His mother told everyone that he'd been literally bouncing with excitement at the event all week and so pleased that his mother told him about it and drove him there. Their experiences of living their gender identities, divided by differences of time and place, were also an occasion for connection. More occasions for such connections— and discussions that wind up showing differences, too—are one way to ensure generations have a way to think together and apart, to create new kinds of social technologies and recognitions. This wouldn't be a new thing. We know that both Compton's Cafeteria Riots, the first organized uprising of gender nonconforming and trans people in the US, and the Stonewall Riots, the uprising of LGBTQ+ people credited with the start of gay liberation in the US, led to the establishment of shelters for trans youth run by older trans people. Shelter and support may come in many different forms but continuing to foster forms of queer trans kinship can help us develop new technologies for recognition and change the spaces in which we meet one another for the better.

# 2

# Working through Concerns and Fears: Tips for Communicating and Messaging about Gender Identity Complexity for Cisgender People

sj Miller

Each person enters into this work at different levels of awareness. Some have a broader and more expansive vocabulary, others may have family, friends, co-workers, or students they have learned with and from, while others have never met someone with a complex gender identity and are unfamiliar with nuance. It's important to recognize that those experiences are common and not just for cisgender folk; trans*[+1] and gender-identity-complex folk are also on a continuum of awareness. Even within these populations, they may not recognize how they contribute to dangerous myths, or lack awareness about how to support others to be allies in the struggle for gender identity self-determination.[2]

The key to leaning into this work is to open up space for people to be who they are and to respond with gentleness, kindness, and respect, and to have patience with, and compassion for, one's self and the other's journeys. The struggle is real for everyone here. In that common recognition, when put together as a team, everyone will have increased capacities to work through questions that arise from each other. Questions might include: how do I work through my fears about misspeaking? What if I mess up; I don't want to offend someone else? What if I don't know what to say, what do I do? And, how do I know what I need to know, when I don't even know what I should know?

To be public about one's gender identity or history of experience shifts one's social positionality from a privileged into a minoritized status as a trespasser of the cisgender body. Yet, to remain quiet, hidden, or to allow oneself to be pushed into the margins in order to comfort the afflicted, should not and can no longer be an option. This work is not about taking care of those who discriminate or who are uncomfortable attending to the needs of vulnerabilized people, or the students this work is aimed toward; it is about how to create and sustain schooling climates that are open and welcoming to the complexity of all gender identities. To truly attend to these changes, we have to reflect on how our own cisgender privilege has been normalized as the appropriate and taken-for-granted body type that evades or is completely off most people's radars. Educators are called to look deeply into themselves, and understand how cisgender privilege maintains and operationalizes schooling environments. Being and staying active in this work are sowing the seeds for change.

Through an immersive "real-time" scenario likely encountered in day-to-day life (e.g., school, work, medical, mental health, etc.), this chapter provides opportunities to both question and address the queries noted above, as well as common presumptions, assumptions, and fears about gender identities. By suggesting practical, visceral, bodily, and response strategies that can open up space for individuals to potentially experience increased capacities for gender identity self-determination, readers are invited and encouraged to wrestle with how their own experiences have played out in prior experiences. Offering misconceptions about the complexity of gender identities,[3] common myths will be dispelled and supportive responses constructed. The significance of these events can proffer a reframing that may be applied to other contexts, especially schools. It is important though to always consider context in any situation because identities, beliefs, values, and ways of being in and reading the world are hardly collapsible, categorizable, or uniform. So, while I provide possible ways through the scenario where aesthetic and efferent responses can occur, their efficacy must be carefully considered before they are applied. Words of caution: efficacy is uneven and can never be decontextualized.

The scenario is "perhaps" (as you will see) between cisgender[4] and non-cisgender people. It begins with a context for cisgender folk: one that goes undetected or may freeze their responses; and one that may create a state of fear, panic, or anxiety, or even move one into a state of hedging. Succeeding the scenario, questions (though others will likely emerge) will guide possible ways to respond by means of discourse stems, body language, sentence patterns, and/or lack thereof.[5] The last part of the scenario will be a broader discussion about the possible impact and significance that the emerging responses can have in the immediate, local, and broader context. A hope is that the scenario will prepare others to be more informed about how to engage with non-cis people while also educating peers about gender identity. A hope is that what emerges from these gleanings will diminish microaggressions and free up the emotional labor that those with complex gender identities are forced to tolerate. Whether an interaction may occur in a split second, twenty seconds, one minute, or longer, so much can be learned from these experiences. But, regardless of the length of time of an event where gendered interactions pose opportunities for challenging presumptions and assumptions—*don't they all for that matter*—it only takes one strategy, in any one moment, to shift structured and often sedimented paradigms into pedagogical opportunities that can pivot thinking, change minds, and, perhaps, lead to enduring outcomes. The indeterminacy of a spread effect can and will transform other environments.

## Target: The Scene

It's the middle of a hot summer's day. Marcos and Michaela are in a mid-size western city. Marcos is queued behind Michaela, and they are standing in/on line[6] in the local Target shopping store, each with over ten items. So, the *regular* check-out line. Standing in/on line and having little to do other than look at the vast array of Tic-Tacs, sugar free gums, trashy magazines, and randomly selected candy bars and the "why on earth are you still selling *Gremlins, Ghostbusters* (the *first* one), and *Dirty Dancing*-like" DVDs, they both seem bored. After exhausting the panorama of these selections, they each look up at the same time, exchange casual glances with no need to converse about their locked-in situation—that sort of: I hate waiting in long lines, this is boring, and I wish this were going faster look—and then look down at their cell phones for the next round of entertainment. They don't know each other.

A person, one might perceive as a woman, sprints up and cuts in front of Michaela and says in a hurried manner, "You don't *mind* do you?" Without a moment to respond, Michaela gives a flip and reluctant head nod and, without much of a chance to say no, surrenders their place in/on line. Michaela tilts their body just enough that Marcos can see Michaela roll their eyes. They then both chuckled half-heartedly, knowing that the Cutter has violated a sacred, but often unspoken, social norm, capitalizing on a privilege historically and still typically conferred to women. Neither needed to speak their feelings: They just knew the Cutter was in the wrong.[7]

## The shoppers

### *Marcos*

Marcos, twenty-eight, is 5 foot 8 inches tall, weighs about 180 pounds and is fit. Marcos is dressed casually, wearing a striped tank top, tan shorts, and brown velcroed sandals. Marcos is well-groomed, has a mustache and goatee, light-brown spiky hair, frosted with white and with a part on the edge of their head, brazen skin, and is Latinx. Based on one's lens of reading gender, others would likely read Marcos as male.

### *Michaela*

Michaela, thirty-two, is taller in stature than Marcos and weighs about the same. Michaela is wearing a long cotton-polyester "ish"-like skirt that has lavender colored swirls, a loose-fitting purple short-sleeved blouse, and tan flats. Michaela is also well-groomed, has a mid-shoulder sassy haircut, and has black hair with purple extensions. Michaela is wearing light make-up, is slender, and black. Based on one's lens, some may perceive Michaela as female, gender non-binary, *or* trans*⁺*.

## The Cutter

The Cutter, for sake of a better word, is in their mid-to-late forties and is shorter than both Michaela and Marcos. The Cutter is wearing a polka-dotted, multi-colored bathing suit, with baggy shorts hiked up to the waistline, and flip flops. The Cutter, who has short sandy-brown hair is wearing a visor and has fly-like lensed sunglasses on their head. The Cutter is sweaty, has a faint scent of coconut suntan lotion and is holding a wallet. While one hand is holding a small cooler, the other holds a floaty device. The Cutter, based on how someone reads or attributes gender identifiers, appears to be a woman. The Cutter is white.

## The ensuing conversation

"Hi, my name is Marcos and I'm wondering if I could ask you a question?"

"Sure, go ahead," says Michaela.

Marcos asks, "When that woman cut in/on line in front of you at the check-out counter, why didn't you say anything?"

"Well, I didn't feel like having a confrontation and I knew the woman would innocently play out some sob story, blah, blah, blah."

*Hold up. Hold up now. You may be thinking, where are you going with this? Well, here's the broader context.*

Scene fades out.

# Reading Bodies at Target

Take a second to think through all of the layers that are activated and co-occurring in simultaneity in this scene. Identities are indivisible, though each person has layers of identities—none can ever be separated from the other, as it is the amalgam of all that makes the individual. What is visible though, and plays a major role in this event, is how gender is presumed, attributed, discerned, positioned, and strengthened. Simultaneously, it is also being questioned, challenged, and critiqued. Might ethnicity, social class, age, clothing, appearance, or any other perceived identifier or privilege also participate? While no identifier can be separated out from anyone, how someone is read is a different story altogether: how one is read is discerned by one's reading of others in the world. I cannot answer that question nor speak for what the reader sees in this scene, I can only present some possible perspectives.

This scene is more layered than first meets the eye. There are indeed many possible ways that this scene can be read and be read through the eyes of each of the players. First, a possibility for how each person was reading the other is described, then followed up with an offering of possible ways that the individuals might have responded. Here is just one decoded possibility....

## Marcos

Marcos reinforces several gendered social norms in this event. First, Marcos positions the Cutter as a cisgender female. For instance, Marcos attributes binary gender identifiers to the statement "you won't mind if I cut" as female because Marcos is connecting and reinforcing how gendered social norms typecast them as more empathic and less possibly confrontational then men. Though unknown, and not presumed here, Marcos *may* think the Cutter is female based on physical appearance and bodily expression; however, this would reside with where Marcos is in how they understand and read gender identity. Lastly, through a shared chuckle with Michaela, Marcos acknowledges that the Cutter has violated a social norm and has used *her* privilege to gain access to check-out in front of them.

It is difficult to know how Marcos reads Michaela. It is discernable that Marcos is kind and thoughtful when they consider how they communicate to Michaela. When Marcos says, "Hi, my name is Marcos and I'm wondering if I could ask you a question?" it is an invitation and not a presumption about Michaela's openness to engage in conversation. Marcos follows up with the question, "When that woman cut in/on line in front of you at the check-out counter, why didn't you say anything?" Marcos draws from their own experience and curiosity likely stemming from other observations of similar events that may have elicited more heated responses. It is difficult to know if Marcos would have responded similarly had the person in front of Marcos been perceived by Marcos as male.

## Michaela

Michaela was put in an awkward position in this scenario and was likely so surprised by the event that they were silenced into response. Without knowing how Michaela self-identifies, the Cutter may have assumed that two women interacting would not provoke or would be less provocative than cutting in front of even who Michaela might have perceived to be male. This response offers revealing insights about where Michaela was in their trajectory of self-awareness.

Michaela, in that moment in Target revealed themselves to be calm. Perhaps this stems from the prior moment of bonding with Marcos around the boring process of waiting in/on line and which may have impacted feeling less agitated by the Cutter's actions. Left to rush into a split-second decision, then likely strengthened by the hurried and persuasive tone of the Cutter, Michaela surrenders a place in/on line. It is difficult to know what instigated that decision, or if it were nothing more than a split second knee-jerk response, but what is clear is that Michaela was not happy about how things played out. Was Michaela reading gender into the situation? Was Michaela desensitized from prior experiences with microaggressions? Or, could it be that Michaela did not want to have a public discussion or even battle about different types of privilege and assumed entitlements converging in this scene such as perceptions of gender, cisgender/cis normativity, class, ethnicity, appearance, etc.?

## The Cutter

Without knowing the Cutter's reason for cutting in/on line and putting themselves in front of Michaela, there are some identifiers that are discernable. Fact: the Cutter was in a hurry about something and regarded that pressure to be expedited into the status of a life and death check-out emergency (think ambulance headlights flashing above). We don't even know what the larger picture looked like in the store. Were there many lines open? Were some longer than others? Was this one closest in proximity to where the Cutter had exited from the aisles? Was the Cutter lazy?

The Cutter may have read Michaela as female and Marcos as male and located themselves in/on line where they thought might elicit the least resistance. Or, perhaps the Cutter sized up each body and felt safer stepping in front of Michaela rather than Marcos for something that may have happened in their past, or fear of a male-appearing person. Or even, perhaps it was as cut and dry as just putting themselves first so they could get out of the store as quickly as possible and be on their way. When the Cutter rhetorically asked Michaela, "You don't *mind* do you?" they were not setting this question up in such a way that the listener would have likely objected. For example, had the Cutter casually walked up to Michaela and asked the same question, it would likely not have produced a silent response. It seemed to be that Michaela's pressured deferment was located both in the hurriedness of the Cutter and a presumed "woman-to-woman" empathic connection, and in assumptions policed onto gender. A casual approach would have likely signaled that the Cutter could have taken their place in/on line and waited. Had the question not been posed as a fast, rhetorical, question that might have conjured an empathic response and rolled out in declarative syntax something like, "I need to get to a swim party. Can I go first?" Or, "I parked my car in the red zone and am in a bit of a hurry," Michaela may have produced a different response altogether. The point here is who even ever really knows anything about anyone's motivations.

## Tar-"jay" *Interrupted*: Possible Responses

Each person in this event responded in ways that speaks to where they are in their own continuum of human awareness. That process is always in flux and sometimes responses are less kind or hospitable then intended to be. Some days we just have bad days, our defenses are down, and it's tough to be as thoughtful or mindful as intended; it's a *symptom*, a condition of just being human.

The descriptions that follow include some possible ways each might have responded. These suggestions for visceral, bodily, and response strategies are meant to help reduce and thwart microaggressions. A hope for this section is to elicit dialogue amongst readers so as to have broader and more far-reaching discussions for the larger contexts of their lives

### Marcos

Marcos might have stepped in and said to the Cutter, "Excuse me, but we were in/on line. Can you help me understand why you assumed it would be acceptable to take your place not only at the front, but to do so in front of person you perceived to be female? What kept you from stepping in front of me, a person you perceived to be male? I also noticed you began to share a story with the person in front of me [though Marcos did not know their name], and it seemed you were using the story in a way that might have provoked empathy and perhaps lessened the impact of cutting in/on line."

## Michaela

After the request to cut in/on line, and without Michaela's body language overtly rejecting the request, Michaela might have said, "Hi there. It seems as though you are in a hurry, however, each of us has been waiting our turn to check out. I am wondering about your reasoning for cutting, in particular, in front of me? I'd appreciate it if you would kindly move to the end of the line, consider another short line, or the self-service line; it looks like there is no waiting?"

## The Cutter

The Cutter might have avoided stirring up frustration had they approached the situation a different way. Upon approaching Michaela and Marcos, they may have uttered the following statement while at the same time positioning their body equidistant between them: "I know it's impolite and impatient of me to ask, and yet, I am in a hurry to return to an event. Would either of you mind if I move to the front of the line? If not, I completely understand."

## Finding Courage to Speak the Truth

These responses may sound kind and empathic. And perhaps they are. Yet, there is so much more than could have been said during this event—so many opportunities that might have played out if each person had the courage and tools to do so. How often, in fact, are we in similar situations but don't speak our truth—what we really want to say? And, what keeps us from doing so? It is likely that first confronting fears could help alleviate some of the anxiety associated with speaking up; but beyond that, having the tools and the confidence to do so is critical. Now, it could be as simple as not wanting to engage because of the emotional labor it entails, but if we are truly committed to making change happen, *living it and leaning into* the work is vital. To only do it sometimes is to reinforce rationales that continue to spatialize normative constructs and beliefs about gender identity. Think of it this way—each and every encounter is indeed an opportunity to make change.

## Strategies in Disrupting a Cisgender Lens

To do this work well, it is helpful to unpack key barriers that often fly under people's radars: cisgender privilege and a cisgender assumption. When left unchallenged and unchecked, cisgender privilege structures the school culture and climate (most spaces for that matter) and sets up potentially dangerous and lasting damaging ideologies that can lead to different types of gender identity violence. Beyond this, addressing fears, body movements, and suggestions of response, strategies are offered to reduce and thwart microaggressions.

A person with a complex gender identity shifts one's social positionality from a privileged into a minoritized status as a trespasser of the cisgender body. This work is not about taking care of those who discriminate or who are uncomfortable attending to the needs of these vulnerabilized students; it is about how to create and sustain schooling climates that are open and welcoming to the complexity of all gender identities.

## Cisgender Privilege

*Cisgender privilege* is the unquestionable entitlement and tendency to move throughout life without the experience of appearance shaming because of one's body or the congruity between how a person looks, acts, and behaves in accordance with how the perceiver reads the perceived. When we perceive someone as cissexual we tend to accept their overall perceived gender as natural and authentic, while disregarding any minor discrepancies in their gender appearance.

Cis privilege typically grants cis people, *without question*, undenied access and recognition to medical care, social environments (e.g., bathrooms, locker or changing rooms, bars, most stores, restaurants, etc.), identity documents (e.g., driver's licenses, social security cards, birth certificates, passports), travel, reflection in the arts, media, texts, language, physical and emotional safety, and privacy. Though not all cisgender people experience these privileges, as there is a continuum of cis people who express complex gender identities, more often than not such entitlements often go unchallenged and unquestioned as it is rooted in our cultural DNA.

Complex gender identities experience just the opposite. When someone is read or clocked (stared at and identified as gender identity complex or trans\*+), their bodies become targets for the possible denial of access to resources and spaces, and of the freedom to move around, and the real possibility of incurring stares, laughs, taunts, physical violence, or even removal from certain environments. For those who are cisgender, consider how simple it is to map and plan out a route, or even not needing to, in order to run mundane errands. Perhaps on this list is to shop for items at the grocery store, pick up dry-cleaning, go to the pet store, return a book to the library, pick up a prescription at the pharmacist, buy lipstick or cologne (depending on who you are) in a department store, or buy all the stuff one *doesn't* need at Target. Even before leaving home, it's not even on the radar to consider how much time one might have to spend in each locale (unless on a time constraint), or who might be encountered in these different arenas. Without some bumps and delays here and there while attending to the list, this excursion is taken for granted. This is how cis privilege works.

Now, for most people that list would be a routine set of tasks and would not be given a second thought. For those who do not benefit from cisgender privilege, that same list is likely to produce a range of anxiety and fear. The list may be narrowed to and structured toward locations that are safe, where the person is *less* likely, not unlikely, to experience stares or mistreatment, and where they can get in and get out as quickly as possible. In fact, depending on an experience in one locale, the list may not even be finished. As a result—and this has come to me through various personal conversations—many people with complex gender identities shop online because of these social conditions, and to avoid the ensuing anxiety.

While I provide a few examples of how cis-bodies are privileged, Appendix A provides a more comprehensive list of how people with complex gender identities or who are trans[*+] are marginalized for their gender identities. As you read this list below consider how these privileges, if left unchallenged, become the regular, ordinary, and daily experiences incurred by students as they move into adulthood; and for students of color, such forms of violence are grossly magnified. In other words, the pipeline for prejudice is well in place and ready for their entrance into a world ready to deride them. The statistics detailing examples of these prejudices would be a book unto itself, so for more specificity about how institutional violence impacts adults who are trans[*+] or have complex gender identities see the following reports: *Transgender Survey: Report on the Experiences of Black Respondents* (Brown and Wilson, 2019); *Transgender Survey: Report on the Experiences of Latino/a Respondents*; and, the *Executive Summary of the Report of the 2015 U.S. Transgender Survey* (James and Salcedo, 2017).

## The Toll of Cisgender Privilege

Research shows that adults who are trans[*+] or have complex gender identities are more at risk than cis-bodies for rejection from families, faith communities, places of work, public accommodations, and health care. They struggle with educational attainment and completion, negative police interactions and mistreatment in prisons, attaining accurate identity documents, and high degrees of emotional, sexual, and physical harassment. When such forms of hatred take over some are forced into sex work for survival, which puts them at even greater risk of experiencing danger. Any of these experiences puts them in close proximity with physical, mental health, and substance abuse issues, homelessness, suicidal ideation, and suicide. Alarmingly, when violence against them escalates, it can and has manifested in the most pernicious, disgusting, and unimaginable forms of murder. Below are a few statistics as archived by the Trans Murdering Monitoring Project (n.d):

- For the average person, there is a *1 in 18,000* chance of being murdered; for people who are trans*++ or have complex gender identities, a *1 in 12* chance; for a trans*++ woman of color, a *1 in 8* chance of being murdered;
- *One in every four* trans*++ people are assaulted; statistics are higher for transwomen of color;
- *One* trans*++ person is horrifically murdered every *twenty-nine* hours by dismemberment, being raped, shot, stabbed, or burned;
- There were 2,016 reported killings of trans*++ and gender diverse people in sixty-five countries worldwide between January 1, 2008 and December 31, 2015, more than 1,500 of which were reported in Central and South America;
- There were twenty-seven recorded deaths in 2016, and twenty-six to twenty-eight (varying reports) in 2017; fourteen were murdered in 2018 and, as of the time of this writing, one person has been murdered in 2019. In each of these cases, two-thirds of each set of statistics refer to women of color.

Violence against poor and working-class women of color who are trans*++ or those who are perceived to have complex gender identities are *the* most at risk for experiencing brutal violence. This epidemic is heightened by a toxic combination of transphobia, racism, and misogyny against the embodiment of these intersections. While systemic forms of racism have and continue to structure the lives of people of color, transmisogyny extends the hatred even further. *Transmisogyny* can be understood as the hatred of women or those who are feminine-identified, the expression of the feminine, or those who are feminine-of-center but not assigned female at birth. It is situated in the assumption that femaleness and femininity are inferior to, and "exist primarily for the benefit of, maleness and masculinity" (Serano, n.d.).

In contrast, the entitlement that cismen have in society tends to carry over to trans*+ men, and those who present as masculine. Seen this way, these individuals, inherit cissexual privilege that tends to be absented for trans*+ women (Serano, 2007). For those who were assigned female at birth and who present as masculine, although they are not immune from transmisogyny, violence against their bodies manifests differently. There are a growing number of studies that reveal that self-harm, such as lacerating and cutting body parts, is on the rise. Some of these individuals have developed a deep hatred for their bodies and feel the need to sever the physical embodiment from the mental. In my case, I covered and am still covering my body with tattoos so I don't have to *see* parts of it. The disidentification between the two provides some, but not entire, relief. Walking in the world with a different and new identity, and experiencing how others respond in ways that are unfamiliar, can elicit and trigger suppressed and/or new emotions. Coming to terms with these new experiences can result in outbursts, rage, and internalized self-hatred. Some become triggered when they come to terms with inheriting male privilege, which can release pent-up rage about their own prior socialization.

The following examples of cis privilege are meant to be viewed as a self-assessment and are written in the first person.

*Clothing*
- There are clothes designed with bodies like mine in mind.
- If I am unable to find clothing that fits me well, I will still feel safe, and recognizable as my gender.

*Healthcare*
- I cannot be denied health insurance on the basis of my gender.
- I expect medical forms to reflect choices regarding my gender.

- I expect that I will not be denied medical treatment by a doctor on the basis of my gender.
- My identity is not considered a mental pathology ("gender dysphoria" in the DSM V) by the psychological and medical establishments.

*Local and National Travel*
- I expect my gender to not unduly affect my ability to travel nationally and internationally.
- If I am asked for a pat down by a TSA agent, I expect it to be done by a person who reflects my gender or will be asked which agent I prefer.
- My gender presentation is legal in all countries.
- I expect that a visa and passport will be sufficient documentation for me to enter any country, however difficult these may be to obtain.

*Media and the Arts*
- Bodies like mine are represented in the media the arts, and in books.
- I can identify with images of my body in movies, plays, shows, etc.
- I see people like me on the news.
- Hollywood accurately depicts people of my gender in films and television, and does not solely make my identity the focus of a dramatic storyline, or the punchline for a joke.

*Offenses*
- Those who wrong me are expected to know that it is hurtful, and are considered blameworthy whether or not they intended to wrong me.
- I have easy access to people who understand that this wrong is not acceptable, and who will support me.
- I have easy access to resources and people to educate someone who wronged me, if I am not feeling up to it.
- If I am being wronged, I can expect that others who are around will notice.

*Physical and Emotional Safety*

- I do not expect someone to question that I am cisgender and if they do, that I would incur violence as a result.
- I do not expect to be demeaned or belittled because I am cisgender.
- I can reasonably assume that I will not be denied services at a hospital, bank, or other institution because the staff does not believe the gender marker on my ID card matches my gender identity.
- I do not expect strangers will ask me what my genitals look like or how I have sex.
- I can walk through the world with little concern for my safety and well-being and do not scan others in fear that I may be assaulted or mocked because of my body and/or appearance.
- If someone else thinks I'm in the wrong bathroom, locker room, or changing room, I am in no danger of verbal abuse, arrest, stares, or physical intimidation.
- I have the ability to flirt, engage in courtship, or form a relationship and not fear that my biological status may be cause for rejection or attack, nor will it cause my partner to question their sexual orientation.
- When I interact with law enforcement, I do not fear interactions with police officers due to my gender identity, nor do I fear that I may be provided differential treatment.
- If I am murdered (or have any crime committed against me), my gender expression will not be used as a justification for my murder ("gay or trans panic"), nor as a reason to coddle the perpetrators.

*Privacy*

- I expect the privacy of my body to be respected in bathrooms, locker rooms, and changing facilities.
- My gender is always an option on a form.
- I am not asked about what my genitalia looks like, or whether or not my breasts are real, what medical procedures I have had, etc.
- I am not asked by others what my "real name" is or was.
- I can reasonably assume that my ability to acquire a job, rent an apartment, or secure a loan will not be denied on the basis of my gender identity/expression.

- I am able to go to places with friends on a whim knowing there will be bathrooms there I can use.

*Sex-segregated facilities*
*I expect access to, and fair treatment within:*
- Domestic violence shelters
- Drug rehabilitation
- Prisons
- Bathrooms, gyms, and locker rooms
- Juvenile justice systems

*Workplace*
- I expect laws banning the creation of a hostile work environment will ban the use of offensive language about me.
- I expect laws to be in place that prevent sexual or gender-type harassment.
- I expect to have a bathroom that I can use without fear of violence, that includes physical or verbal intimidation, stares, or ridicule.

This list, when taken together with the reports named above, provides only a snapshot of some of the unchecked and/or uninterrupted ways that cisgender privilege perpetuates violence; this should leave little question as to why this must be addressed, disrupted, and stopped early on in students' educational experiences. There is so much work to do!

## Cisgender Assumption

When students cross onto school property, their bodies and minds become unknowing participants in a roulette of gender identity norms (Miller, 2016). As this occurs, students gender identity self-determination is taken away as these norms are inscribed onto them. The *cisgender assumption* is the condition and practice of reinforcing cisgender privilege, cisnormativity and the cisgender/cissexual body. Whether unknowingly or with intention, this contributes to the invalidation, delegitimization, marginalization, *and* erasure of complex gender identities. Think about how many superintendents, principals, and other key school stakeholders have no clue about how they reinforce these assumptions. Consider this process beginning in pre-school and then extended into elementary, middle and secondary schools, and even into university settings. Consider the impact that this may have not only on those students, but on every other student who is being conditioned and primed to recycle, stain, and blemish the souls of all complex gender identities. As this condition continues, everyone is left with diminished capacities to create and inform change. It is important for us to remember that we live in a time we never made; gender and gender identity norms predate our existence; norms operate to pathologize and delegitimize them; students have rights to their own gender identity legibility; binary views on gender identity are potentially damaging; students are all entitled to the same basic human rights; and, they should be free to navigate the schooling process without fear for their well-being. However, often through no fault of their own, many educators carry the cisgender assumption into schooling practices. Our job, then, is to unlearn the assumption, negotiate to the extent to which we allow this assumption to go unchallenged, and cultivate new practices that not only move away from normalizing the cis-body, but ensure that schooling practices presume that multiple identities co-occur all the time. I refer to this as the *both/and*—yep, they can both exist! Beginning with the notion that identities are on a continuum, never fixed or static, but indeterminate, can silence the ubiquity of the norm from continuing to pathologize bodies.

## Cissexualism and Cissexism

If the cisgender assumption is the condition and practice, unknowingly or with deliberate intention, of erasing complex gender identities— yes, believe it or not people do this—*cissexualism* is the impact of the prejudice by which all gender-normative-appearing bodies are always assumed not to be trans*++. Binary thinking continues to be pervasive in language, gender, and sexuality research, which then narrows, constrains, and essentializes sex *and* gender. These limitations impact what could otherwise expand emerging views, epistemologies, methodologies, and analyses, leading to shifts in awareness about the indeterminacy of gender identity both in and out of school. Rather than accepting binaries as inevitable, we must change our thinking in our approach to this process so we can produce suggestions that foster opportunities, leading to possibilities for distributable and equitable outcomes (Miller, 2019).

Cissexism continues this pipeline of deficitized perspectives about complex gender identities and locks into place cis- and gender-identity normativity. *Cissexism* is the unchecked tendency to view trans*++ people and those with complex gender identities as less legitimate than cissexuals. It is deeply rooted in the institutional structures that govern bodies and privileges cis-bodies, renders them as unquestionable, unmarked, and taken for granted. For example, if all cis people stayed home for a day, a week, or a year, cis privilege remains intact. For cisgender privilege and its subsequent trajectory to be destroyed, requires a sustained commitment to shifting policies, mindsets, localities, and practices. Students deserve this, and it's long overdue.

## School Through the Eyes of Students with Complex Gender Identities

Students with complex gender identities seem to express the embodiment of gender critique more visibly than in times past. While the school system is dependent on, and set up through, a neoliberal design, their dexterity in negotiating the politics that seek to police them amplify their resistance to assimilation. Though the politics of neoliberalism are seemingly troubling, students are re-navigating their creativity and their identities in response to these polemic relationships. Such obstacles, though, are priming students to become agents of change. While shifts in federal, state, and local policies do impact students' rights in schools, it has galvanized growing student-led coalitions and, in some ways, helped them find the courage to speak up and fight back. Legal changes, therefore, that impact students who are trans*+ and have complex gender identities have propelled front-facing issues targeted at these minoritized students and entered into mainstream discussions.

Even with changes in the educational system, these students must simultaneously hold up two images of the self: the internal and the external—while always trying to compose and reconcile their identity. Du Bois (1903), was indignantly concerned with how black recognition forced a split of consciousness between the internal and external worlds, and argued that such disintegration of the two generates internal strife and confusion about a positive sense of self-worth. For students, then, who live outside of the gender identity binary and challenge traditionally entrenched forms of gender identity expression, they too experience this pernicious and debilitating double-consciousness.

Age dependent, many students who are trans*+ or have complex gender identities mentally map out their days before they leave home. Some leave home for school with an appearance that evades derision or ridicule with bags containing different clothes, make-up, shoes, hair gel/spray, jewelry, etc., that they can change into in order to feel comfortable about how they look at school. And, before they arrive home, they strip off the identity and enter back into the world of the double-consciousness (Du Bois, 1903). Some are forced, out of the need for safety and protection, to pre-plan which door, hallway, bathroom, or locker room to enter or not to enter. They are forced to think about who to avoid, where not to go, where not to eat, and what not to say. In fact, it is not uncommon for many of these students to end up with urinary tract infections because of fear of harassment in bathrooms. Sometimes, they have to act, dress or behave in false or incomplete ways to mollify or placate others' anxieties in order to avoid being bullied. They are often forced to spend more time taking care of others' anxieties than focusing on their own well-being. It is difficult to do well in school or to think about the future when time is spent trying to figure out how to survive daily, and this situation often leaves these students completely bankrupt.

## How a Recognition Gap and Identity Erasure Impact Students

Many educators are aware that students who are trans\*+ and have complex gender identities are made vulnerable to experiencing myriad forms of bullying in schools. Considered as microaggressions, bullying manifests in visible, invisible, and absented forms. When these students fail to be named, recognized, or legitimated by schooling practices they face the possibility of being erased. Such erasure forecloses a potential expanding of awareness about these bodies and can lead to rationales that perpetuate gender-identity-based violence. In other words, when the system fails to recognize students on a continuum of gender identities that are complex, they are *made* vulnerable to experiencing a cascade of dangerous negative habitus-related consequences. In order to change this, we must minimize the discontinuities between literacy learning and learning literacy between, inside, and outside of school contexts.

### Disconcerting Facts about Students Who Have Complex Gender Identities.

Non-disaggregated data from research by grade level reveals that students who have complex gender identities experience higher and more disproportionate rates than their lesbian, gay, and bisexual peers of bullying and violence, punitive disciplinary action, truancy, dropping out, lowered academic completion, performance, GPAs, mental health and substance issues, pushout into the school-to-prison pipeline and the foster care system, homelessness, and suicidal ideation.[2] For these students, statistics from the GLSEN's (2016) report, *Separation and Stigma: Transgender Youth & School Facilities* revealed:

- 75 percent of transgender students felt unsafe at school because of their gender or gender expression;
- 61 percent of genderqueer students and students with another gender felt unsafe at school because of their gender or gender expression;
- 65 percent of transgender students say that they experience verbal harassment based on their gender expression, 25 percent are physically harassed, and 12 percent are physically assaulted at least sometimes at school;
- 70 percent of transgender students avoid their school's bathrooms;
- 75 percent of transgender and genderqueer students had experienced some form of discrimination at school (e.g., bullying, refusal to use claimed name or pronoun, misrecognition of identities on forms and questionnaires, absence of discussions in classes attending to complex gender identities, questions about body parts and gender);
- 45.2 percent of transgender and 48.9 percent of students with non-binary gender identities had experienced exclusionary discipline and criminal sanctions (GLSEN, 2016);
- 3.5 percent of transgender students and 3.1 percent of those with another gender identity reported more overall contact with the juvenile processing system as a result of school discipline compared to their LGBQ cisgender peers; and
- With each suspension or disciplinary action, a student's odds of not graduating high school increases by 20 percent and the chance of their attending post-secondary education decreases by 12 percent.

Warranting urgent and immediate concern, and this cannot be emphasized enough, is the fact that students of color who are trans*+ and have complex gender identities, when combined with a queer sexual orientation, experience *the* highest rates of school violence (James, Brown, and Wilson, 2017; James and Salcedo, 2017). Accounting for both groups, more than 50 percent will have made at least one suicide attempt by their twentieth birthday. Attempts and completion rates of suicide for all trans*+ and gender-identity-complex students continue to surpass those in *any* population of teens to date.

## Strategies for Disruption of Presuming Cisnormativity

While strides have been made in policies that support students with complex gender identities, there is a glaring absence of the inclusion of multi-disciplinary curricula (e.g., texts, histories, media, art, science, math, trailblazers, foreign language, technology, etc.) and professional development that embraces its complexities. Though gender identity has been thrust into mainstream attention, schools have yet to catch up with the rapid pace at which students are self-determining their gender identities. For these concerns to be addressed, changed, and embedded into schooling practices, will take a critical mass of unlearning and unschooling around how bodies that are inconsistent with the existing ideologies are positioned as inferior. To not do this work reinforces cisnormativity and designates differences in gender identities as inferior.

# Both/And

To have the belief and practice of the both/and is to simultaneously teach about the lack of privileging of the cis-body and to show how equity co-exists between the complexities of all gender identities. This departure from educational convention posits the educational system as more expansive and embracing. The both/and is not a doing away with binaries or discarding them from our lived experiences; rather it is advocating for a more complex and contextually grounded engagement with the binary. We may be somewhat limited in our current understanding about gender identity self-determination, but embracing the both/and can foster and galvanize personal, social, and cultural shifts. We know that people engage in a number of linguistic practices outside the binary to self-define their gender identities, but such a rejection of the mutual exclusivity of binaries does not mean that dualities are not necessarily opposites outcomes (Miller, 2019).

The solutions about how to attend to this work, though, are staring us in the face each and every day we work in schools; the students are the walking, breathing, embodiment of literacy, and the literacy learning that needs to be enculturated. Considered this way, literacy is how one is read by the world and how others come to understand that embodiment. While this can entail conventional definitions of literacy such as acquiring different modes to communicate, gender-identity-situated literacy refers to how students with complex gender identities are legitimated by their own inventions and lenses of language vis-à-vis reading, writing, speaking, gesturing, validating, etc., and how others come to learn literacy through those inventions and reinventions. As such forms of literacy and literacy practices become part of the schooling context everyone expands in their awareness of the indeterminacy of literacy and literacy learning.

If the educational system were to recognize the co-existence of students' bodies as literacy learning, and fold in the both/and of the cis- and complex-gender-identity body as constitutive of the other, then shifts in mindsets, pedagogy, culture, and climate are likely to occur. It may not be as easy it seems, but it is our job to listen and learn from and with our students. As both a lens and a practice, the both/and can cease erasure from sedimenting any deeper. Understanding gender identity as trans-sectional is a critical strategy that can disrupt and generate more expansive ways of thinking about gender-identity self-determination in all contexts.

## Gender Identity is Trans-sectional

The scene that played out in Target is indeed deeply layered: most situations are. A variety of factors are always in play at any given moment. In fact, many, if not most, are invisible and indeterminate. We can never truly walk in someone's skin or know what another is thinking or feeling: nor can we ever disentangle the braids of any person's identities that co-exist and are impacted in unison. One way, though, to disentangle and try to make sense of the layers of layers, is through a trans-sectional lens (Miller, 2019). I hope that when reflecting on this chapter, your critique becomes a rich opportunity to dialogue with others.

Identities are never singular and cannot be collapsed into any one single identifier—they are indivisible. While an identifier might be visible or heightened on a body, there are always other identities swirled and comingling inside a person. As people interact with others and learn about themselves, their sense of self and ways of understanding the world is in constant motion—and far from static. This swirling is what I call trans-sectional; a coming together of multiple forms of identities always in perpetual deconstruction and construction and identified by their indeterminate integration and ever-shifting amalgamation of identities. Trans-sectional is the generating and embedding of new knowledges and recognitions of self-awareness that both shake up and wake up contexts. It presumes that identities are unfixed yet stabilized by the act of self-determining one's gender identity.

To enter into the notion that identities are trans-sectional requires capacious and fundamental shifts in how to approach identity work. It helps to consider that trans-sectional cannot be codified or be capturable and that its very nature is to undo and resist categorization. Trans*+ and complex gender identities complicate how we understand their positions, and Mayo (2017) suggests that a queering of identities undoes, dismantles, and resists categorization. In fact, the destabilization of gender identity amplifies it as a resource for escaping the binary. Trans-sectional, therefore, is a form of disentangling from, and blurring the lines of, a gender identity binary. When people resist exclusionary practices that seek to reinforce gender identity normativity, they participate in forms of resistance that create and inspire forms of new knowledge to grow. These changes carry tremendous potential for the next iterations of gender identities to be recognized. Their resistance can reposition educators to make a *trans-sectional turn*, a shift in educational contexts that galvanizes new actions. This turn can inspire how to negotiate new forms of recognition of ethnic, gendered, classed, linguistic, able-bodied, and sexual diversity subjectivities, to name a few, as they shift over time and in different contexts (Miller, 2019).

## Gender Identity is Trans-cultural

Trans-cultural is the conceptualization for complex gender-identity formation. It accounts for the trans-sections, or *movements* of bodies, technologies, spaces, times, contexts, and cultural identifiers that embody ethnic, linguistic, and literacy practices that produce both material and symbolic meanings (e.g., literacy, appearance, recognition of expressions). Trans-cultural then is the trans-section, i.e., the rhizome or networked space, whereby relationships intersect, are concentric, do not intersect, can be parallel, nonparallel, perpendicular, obtuse, and fragmented. It is both an invisible and visible space that embodies all of the forces co-constructing gender identities that traverse borders of space, time, and technology, and that carves out and generates pathways into different contexts where gender identities are formed and generated. As gender identities transect, they continue to be shaped by different social configurations and dynamics, thus inheriting new qualities, and new ways of being recognized by themselves and others. When complex gender identities move across different physical, material, and symbolic borders, the movement activates and fortifies (although temporally) new gender identity formations.[8]

## Confronting Fears

Below is a starter set for addressing fears. Some of this work can be done individually and some collaboratively. In no particular order, these strategies can help how to work through some concerns and build more confidence for leaning into the work. Beyond these, other concerns may be related to unknown factors such as what policies say and don't say, or how federal, state, municipal, and local districts unknowingly or intentionally set up discriminatory practices, or even having access to information that is false, misleading, or dated. Ultimately, since concerns are context-bound, are culturally and linguistically specific, and based on level of awareness, attending to these questions and subsequent approaches is a matter of need, demand, and preference. It might be useful to connect with others while working through some of these starting points, which will likely spur additional queries. In fact, consider jotting down some thoughts, aggregating responses, thematically organizing them, and creating an action plan. To begin the process, remember to first remind yourself that *you can have courageous conversations.*

Consider these questions:

- Where do these fears come from?
- What can I do to address my fears?
- What hinders me from engaging more deeply in the work?
- Who is vehemently outspoken about the work?
- What can I do when others oppose the work?
- How do I build my confidence?
- How do I respond to students who have questions about gender identity, what resources do I need, and what are effective strategies to practice my responses?
- How do I assess what students need to feel safe, affirmed, and recognized?
- How do I respond to peers, colleagues, or the every-common person I meet when they have questions about gender identity, what resources do I need, and what are effective strategies to practice my responses?
- How can I continue to find resources?
- Who is doing the work that can support efforts to strengthen larger awareness and understanding?
- How can I speak to caregivers who have oppositional views?
- What can I do in my own institution?

- How can I work with leadership who has oppositional views?
- What can I do or draw from in the community to support efforts by my institution?
- What can I do at the local state level?
- How can local clergy support these efforts, especially when others have oppositional perspectives?
- How can I network and build a school-wide, community-wide, or state-wide coalition?
- What are some strategies to respond to the every-person in my common day-to-day interactions whether directed at me or someone else, when what is said about gender identity is either untrue, prejudiced, and/or malicious and/or perpetuates stereotypes?
- Now, where, or when do I begin?

While this list may seem overwhelming, remember Rome was not built in a day, and this work is life-long, for *all* of us. Identities will continue to shift, but as people remain open, listen, and are contextually responsive, relationships between cis, non-cis, and those with complex gender identities can pave the way into a gentler, kinder, and more open humanity.

## Strategies: Positioning the Body

Bodies show comfort and discomfort, whether unknowingly or not, about how people feel about the other. For instance, typically, leaning into a conversation, positioning and angling the body toward the other reflects a heightened interest in what the other says. Likewise, direct eye contact, nodding, and making small, seemingly affirming utterances (e.g., aha, I hear you, mmm, etc.) when the other speaks shows interest and concern. While these movements don't always reflect interest, they, more often than not, often indicate care and engagement. These qualities may both initiate and invite another to be more open with their responses, and/or indicate that some form of connection is present.

In contrast, when a body is angled away from another, it may indicate lack of comfort, distrust, or feigned indifference. For instance, sometimes when a body is positioned away from, such that the angle slants, rather than toward the other, there may be either an obvious slant or a more subtle distance. Eye contact may be inconsistent, utterances or tones may sound unconvincing or disinterested, and bodily movements (e.g., twirling hands or rings, tapping a foot, moving a shoulder or leg) may seem agitated or fidgety. One of the most obvious signs of discomfort—and this happens to gender non-binary people more often than not—is when coming out as trans*++ to another, the other person's body shifts away. This can take the form of leaning away, moving a shoulder, arching back, or making a sudden hand or leg movement. Such acts can signal to trans*++ and those with complex gender identities that the other is not safe to talk to and impact, delimit, and foreclose further conversation.

Of course, these examples are not hard and fast and there are always exceptions; so, take from these examples some signifiers that can spur and lead to creating spaces and opportunities for people to disclose who they are so more authentic conversations can be had.

Bodily tips that demonstrate care and understanding to those with complex gender identities:

- Lean in to discussions
- Nod your head and affirm comments
- Make eye contact
- Keep your body still
- Position your body horizontally while communicating
- Smile and/or be sure your facial expressions reflect kindness

## Gender Identity Complexities Framework (GICF)

My prior work attended to teaching, affirming, and recognizing students' gender and sexuality in literacy practices in order to support their self-determination and manifest gender and sexual diversity justice through the Queer Literacy Framework (QLF), paired with axioms (Miller, 2015b). The QLF then moved specifically into strategies advocating for transgender students (Miller, 2016) and now has pivoted into suggestions and offerings that advocate for the complexities of gender identity (Miller, 2019).

The GICF[9] provides strategies for how to approach the classroom, construct lessons and present possibilities for shifting educational and various other contexts and environments. The GICF, similar to the QLF, is guided by axioms and comprises ten principles with subsequent commitments for stakeholders who advocate for the complexity of gender identity in pre-K–12th grade, university settings, and beyond. The framework is underscored by the notion that lives have been structured through an inheritance of a political, gendered, economic, social, religious, and linguistic system with indissoluble ties to a cisnormative heteropatriarchy. This is not to suggest a dismissal from (a)gender identity categories altogether, which refers to the rejection of gender as a biological or social construct and the refusal to identify with gender, but to move into an expansive and open-ended paradigm that refuses to close itself or be narrowly defined, and that strives to shift and expand views that can account for a continuum of evolving (a)gender identities and differential bodied realities. Though the framework was built to support students, it can be applied and adapted within myriad educational spaces, work environments, and daily interactions. I would suspect that if the individuals in Target had prior experience with some these suggestions, and felt comfortable doing so, the event would have likely played out differently.

First and foremost, student's voices and expressions of gender identities need to be heard, affirmed, and recognized. The GICF can support your work while validating, recognizing, and advocating for students. The framework is intended to be an autonomous, ongoing, nonhierarchical tool within educational spaces; it is not something someone does once and moves away from. Rather, the principles and commitments should work alongside other tools and perspectives within dispositions, curricula, documents, and policy. An intention of the framework is that it can be applied and taken up across multiple educational genres, disciplines (e.g., lessons, pedagogy, codes of conduct, posters and signs, local and district policy, etc.), and contexts, and its spreading across different contexts can expand awareness about complex gender identities. Moving into the GICF, axioms underscore the beliefs that guide the principles and commitments. Discussing these axioms (see Figure 2.1) and unpacking the language within contexts with *all* stakeholders can cultivate a deeper awareness about how some people may not be aware that they enact microaggressions and create unsafety for students.

> ➢ We live in a time we never made; gender and gender identity norms predate our existence;
> ➢ Non-gender and gender identity "differences" have been around forever but norms operate to pathologize, invalidate and delegitimize them;
> ➢ Children's self-determination is taken away early when gender and gender identity are inscribed onto them. Their bodies/minds become unknowing participants in a roulette of gender and gender identity norms;
> ➢ Children have rights to their own (a)gender and gender identity legibility;
> ➢ Binary views on gender and gender identity are potentially damaging;
> ➢ Gender and gender identity must be dislodged/unhinged from sexuality;
> ➢ Humans have agency;
> ➢ We must move away from pathologizing beliefs that police humanity;
> ➢ Humans deserve positive recognition and acknowledgment for who they are;
> ➢ We are all entitled to the same basic human rights; and,
> ➢ Life should be livable for all.

**Figure 2.1** Axioms for Gender Identity Complexities Framework

Building from these axioms, then, stakeholders who practice this framework have increased capacities to shift mindsets and physical environments as they apply the various principle(s) identified in Figure 2.2.

Embedded in the framework are suggestions for communicating with stems and discourse patterns. Similar to bodily expressions, there are discourse stems and sentence patterns that demonstrate supportive

| Principles | Commitments Advocating for Complex Gender Identities |
| --- | --- |
| 1. Refrains from possible presumptions that students ascribe to a gender or their gender identity is readily discernable | Stakeholders who advocate for complex gender identities never presume that students have a gender or understand how students self-identify |
| 2. Understands gender as a construct which has and continues to be impacted by trans-secting expressions of gender identity (e.g., social, historical, material, cultural, economic, linguistic, religious) | Stakeholders who advocate for complex gender identities are committed to actively push back against gender and gender identity constructs and provide opportunities to explore, engage and understand how they are constructed. |
| 3. Recognizes that masculinity and femininity constructs are assigned to gender and gender identity norms and are situationally performed | Stakeholders who advocate for complex gender identities challenge gender and gender identity norms and stereotypes and actively support students' various and multiple performances of gender and expressions of gender identity. |
| 4. Understands gender and gender identity as flexible and dexterous | Stakeholders who advocate for complex gender identities are mindful about how specific discourse(s) can reinforce gender and gender identity norms, and purposefully demonstrate how gender and gender identity are fluid, or exist on a continuum, shifting over time and in different contexts. |
| 5. Opens up spaces for students to self-define with claimed (a) genders, (a)pronouns, or names | Stakeholders who advocate for complex gender identities invite students to self-define and/or reject claimed or preferred gender, name, and/or pronoun. |

| | |
|---|---|
| 6. Engages in ongoing critique of how gender and gender identity norms are reinforced in literature, media, technology, art, history, science, math, policy, etc., | Stakeholders who advocate for complex gender identities provide ongoing and deep discussions about how society is gendered and cisnormative, and invite students to actively engage in analysis of cultural texts and disciplinary discourses. |
| 7. Understands how neoliberal principles reinforce and sustain compulsory heterosexism; how cissexism secures homophobia, and cissexualism; and how gendering and a cisgender assumption secure bullying and transphobia | Stakeholders who advocate for complex gender identities understand and investigate structural oppression and how heterosexism and cissexism sustain body-type violence, and then generate meaningful opportunities for students to become embodied change agents, to be proactive against, or to not engage in bullying behavior. |
| 8. Understands that (a)gender and gender identity trans-sect with other identities (e.g. sexual orientation, culture, language, age, religion, social class, body type, accent, height, ability, disability, and national origin) and informs students' beliefs and thereby, actions | Stakeholders who advocate for complex gender identities do not essentialize students' identities, but recognize how trans-sections of sexual orientation, culture, language, age, religion, social class, body type, accent, height, ability, disability, immigration status, and national origin, inform students' beliefs and thereby, actions. |
| 9. Advocates for equity across all expressions of (a)gender and gender identities | Stakeholders who advocate for complex gender identities do not privilege one belief or stance, but advocate for equity across all expressions of (a)gender and gender identities. |
| 10. Believes that students who identify on a continuum of gender identities deserve to learn in environments free of bullying and harassment | Stakeholders who advocate for complex gender identities make their positions known, when first hired, to students, teachers, administrators and school personnel and take a stance when any student is bullied or marginalized, whether explicitly or implicitly, for their (a)gender identities. |

**Figure 2.2** Gender Identity Complexities Framework: Promoting (A)Gender Identity Self-Determination and Justice

Source: Modified version of "Figure 1: A Queer Literacy Framework Promoting (A)Gender and (A)Sexuality Self-Determination and Justice." Originally published on p. 42 of *English Journal* 104.5 (2015). Copyright 2015 by the National Council of Teachers of English. Used with permission.

ways to engage with people who have complex gender identities. The following examples can be applied to many contexts, age ranges, cultures, linguistic groups, and people with disabilities amongst other identities, though adjustments should always be accounted for. The framework will be most effective and beneficial to others if entered into based on background knowledge and comfort level. The framework should be approached with a unifying presupposition: assume nothing about *any* aspect of their identities.[10]

## Application of Gender Identity Complexities Framework

For each principle, I provide examples and additional appendices that can be drawn up and applied in classes, meetings, and interactions with others. The examples are general enough to be applied for any educational level, discipline, and context. Since educators know their contexts best, adapting principles to the context is critical and should align with students' cultural, classed, and linguistic backgrounds. In addition, if English is not their first language, translating the framework for each population is important (*Teaching Affirming and Recognizing Trans and Gender Creative Youth* has been translated into Spanish, see Miller, 2016). In some languages, terms are not translatable, some are gendered, and in others, cannot be pronounced. In any of these cases, adapting the framework with colleagues and/or students will provide rich and deep discussions about the social construction and policing of gender, and opportunities to imagine, invent, and self-determine one's gender identity.

**Principle 1.** *Refrains from possible presumptions that students ascribe to a gender or that their gender identity is readily discernable.*

Example 1:

When stakeholders approach any context, they can keep stay mindful to not presume *anything* about anyone. Regardless of how a student dresses or behaves, to place any type of identifier on a student is already setting both the educator and the student to be framed within a cascade of indexical binaries.

Specific questions for both examples might include:

- Ask students where notions of gender arise. Ask them how such notions are reinforced. Ask, do people have to "be" or "have a gender".
- Ask students what ideas, concepts, behaviors, mannerisms, activities, dress, feelings, occupations, seem to be identified with gender or gender identity. Ask them for examples in society where gender seems fluid and non-descript.
- Ask for examples where people seem to be (a)gender or gender flexible.
- Ask students what makes gender and gender identity matter.
- Ask what happens to people who are gender flexible or who seem to express themselves differently from the sex they were assigned.

Example 2:

Stakeholders can put up posters and images in classrooms and hallways that reflect myriad representations of identities. When only images appear in materials or in hallways with cisgender or gender normative people, stakeholders can have discussions about why and how certain identities appear more often than others.

**Principle 2.** *Understands gender as a construct that has been and continues to be impacted by transecting expressions of gender identity (e.g., social, historical, material, cultural, economic, linguistic, religious).*

Example 1:

Stakeholders can root conversational and pedagogical approaches to students that respect and honor their multiple co-existing identities *and* their indeterminacy. In daily conversations, moving away from monological or closed-question approaches and into an unbounded space can invite others to experience self-determination. Questions might begin with, "Tell me about your experience," "How does this impact you?" "Are you affected by any changes in local or national policies?" "How do you feel about what you just read or saw?"

Example 2:

Stakeholders can encourage students to look at how they position others. They can invite conversations about how certain rights are limited or denied based on an identity, yet how other identities grant privilege and access. This can contribute to their seeing how their own identities are complicated in relationship to education, policies, and the built environment.

**Principle 3.** *Recognizes that masculinity and femininity constructs are assigned to gender and gender identity norms and are situationally performed.*

Example 1:

Stakeholders can approach others with the mindset that there is an array of identities and all identities are constructed. Considered this way, identities are never masculine or feminine or gendered because they were assigned identifiers in a different historical context and for specific purposes. Building from here, stakeholders can hold space for inviting in how to unlearn common positioning and move away from the policing of expectations associated with how gender and gender identity tend to be positioned as masculine or feminine.

Example 2:

When in conversation with others, strategies can be pulled from Example 1. For example, students can be encouraged to question others, and to reflect on what they see in the media and who is reinforcing these norms. They can ask others to revisit their own histories and reflect on at what point in their lives they felt they were a gender or were a particular gender identity. Pushing one step further, they can ask how those views changed over time and what instigated those changes.

**Principle 4.** *Understands gender and gender identity as flexible and dexterous.*

Example 1:

Stakeholders can be in constant conversation about the flexibility of gender and gender identity. In everyday parlance, stakeholders can practice how the terms they use for gender and gender identity position others. When they catch themselves, they can rephrase the term and say, "Oops, I didn't mean to assume an identity." They can also remain open and non-judgmental about students who shift in their appearance.

Example 2:

Stakeholders can speak about gender and gender identity in supportive ways. When speaking with students, they can be mindful to move away from binaries for anyone. They can take up the both/and approach on assignments and perspectives, and ask students to remind them when they may inadvertently position someone. The mutual effort in and of itself can provide opportunities for ongoing discussions.

**Principle 5.** *Opens up spaces for students to self-define with claimed (a)genders, (a)pronouns, or names.*

Example 1:

The "Get to Know Me" allows students to privately reveal their *current*[11] claimed name, (a)gender identity (i.e., gender identity or absence thereof), and (a)pronouns (i.e., pronouns or absence thereof), and with an option to note if they want these identities publicly acknowledged (see Figure 2.3 and Appendix B). For the student who does not want others to know about particular identities, but is comfortable sharing that part of the self with the educator, the educator can respond on assignments with comments that recognize the student's true name, (a)gender identity, and or (a)pronoun.

Stakeholders can put up pronoun posters as a visible affirmation of gender identity self-determination (see Figure 2.4 and Appendix C).

My assigned name is _____ and my claimed name (leave blank if they are the same) is _____. My assigned sex is _____ but my CURRENT, claimed (a)gender identity (leave blank if they are the same) is _____. The pronouns people use when referring to me include _____ but my CURRENT, claimed (a)pronoun is/are_____.

In class I prefer you to use (please circle) *assigned* or *claimed* <u>name,</u> *assigned* or *claimed* <u>(a)pronouns,</u> but on my assignments, you can use (please circle) *assigned or claimed* <u>name</u> and *assigned* or *claimed* <u>(a)pronouns.</u>

**Figure 2.3** Get to Know Me

Do **you** use *pronouns*?

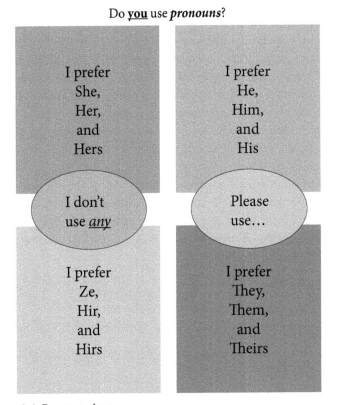

I prefer
She,
Her,
and
Hers

I prefer
He,
Him,
and
His

I don't
use *any*

Please
use...

I prefer
Ze,
Hir,
and
Hirs

I prefer
They,
Them,
and
Theirs

**Figure 2.4** Pronoun chart

Example 2:

Another way stakeholders can affirm and recognize students is to post placards in the classroom and hallways that affirm gender identity and inclusivity (see Figure 2.5 and Appendix D) and make gender/agender identity recognition part of the ordinary classroom experience. Appendix E provides a lengthy and growing list of terms students are cataloguing online, which names their self-determined genders, gender identities, pronouns, and romantic orientations.

**Principle 6.** *Engages in ongoing critique of how gender and gender identity norms are reinforced in literature, media, technology, art, history, science, math, policy, etc.*

Example 1:

Stakeholders can support students to challenge how gender and gender identity are represented in various genres. For example, students can participate in a number of gender identity and cisgender audits (and create others) in order to determine how binary identities are reinforced in any given twenty-four hours. The purpose of these activities are to draw attention to the aggregate and often unconscious reinforcement of beliefs about normative identities across a week, a month, a year, a lifetime, etc., and how such messages reinforce dominant perceptions. During this time, students can be asked to chart their observations from when they wake up until the next day, what they see, what was said, and who was reinforcing the identity. They can share their findings and fill in data on butcher paper, and do a gallery walk to observe the quantity of responses from those twenty-four hours (see Appendix F).

Example 2:

Stakeholders can ask questions that challenge others to think about how gender identities are represented. Some useful prompts include:

• How are binary gender identities reinforced in a movie, talk show, the news, or TV show?

# Inclusive Space

This space
***RESPECTS***
all aspects of people including age, gender, race,
ethnicity, religion/no religion, national origin,
immigration status, language, education, marital status,
body size, political affiliation/philosophy, (a)sexual
orientation, (a)gender identity/expression and
creativity, physical and mental ability, social-economic
status, genetic information, medical status, veteran
status, and the indeterminate.

**Figure 2.5** Inclusive space sign

- How are gender identity binaries reinforced in educational context (other classes, school policies, messages, posters, sports, etc.)? How are these binaries socially policed?

- How are binary gender identities reinforced in different disciplines and genres/sub genres within technology, art, history, radio, podcasts, music, literature, science, math, sports, policy, etc.? How are binary gender identities socially policed?

- In which of these courses are challenges against binary gender identities noticed and what has resulted or been discovered from the push back?

- Which authors explore social policing and reinforcement of binary gender identities and what has been learned from those texts?

- How are binary gender identities reinforced in texts across different aspects of characters' lives and what is the impact? How are those socially policed in the text?

- Provide examples of how binary gender identities are interrupted and disrupted?

- Describe observations about challenges to binary gender identities and what has been learned? What has been the social impact of this awareness?

- Describe connections and draw inferences about complex binary gender identities between oneself and textual characters and artists, musicians, athletes, media personalities, religious figures, politicians, friends or family, and in any academic discipline, etc. What have they experienced? How were they treated?

**Principle 7.** *Understands how neoliberal principles reinforce and sustain compulsory heterosexism; how cissexism secures homophobia, and cissexualism; and how gendering and a cisgender assumption secure bullying and transphobia.*

Example 1:

For any stakeholder (students included), introductions and greetings disrupt assumptions around gender and gender identity. Consider using this greeting:

- "Hi, nice to meet you. My current claimed name is ___ and my current claimed pronoun (or, in some cases, [a]pronoun) is/are she/her/hers___. How would you like me to refer to you?"

Depending on one's familiarity with another, they might add:

- "My current claimed gender identity (or, in some cases, [a]gender) is/are ___."

These interactions may invite a conversation around gender identity that recognizes and signals to others that gender identity is on an ever-expanding spectrum. When someone says they are cisgender they demonstrate their awareness that trans*[+] and complex-gender identities exist. If someone doesn't know what cisgender means, it may invite a conversation. This can lead to expanding its use and ongoing impact. For instance:

- "Currently, I am a (fill in sexual orientation) heteroflexible, (fill in gender identification) cisgender (fill in gender identity) female."

Example 2:

Stakeholders can use the first person singular they, them/themself, their, theirs, and themselves[12] when referencing someone's identity. For example,

- "The student stood up and went to *their* desk."
- "Somebody got in their car, but *they* did not know where to drive."
- "They grabbed *their* jacket before *they* left."
- "They refer to *themselves* as Marcos."

Or, stakeholders might consider not using any pronouns and solely rely on the person's name. For example:

- "Sam stood up and Sam went out the door."
- "Kaneesha decided that Kaneesha had enough and left."

Example 3:

A teacher assumes the cisnormative social positioning of a body or gender identity when they say, "Hey, guys, take out your notebooks." When a student corrects that teacher and responds with, "We are not all guys, and when you say that you position everyone to be male; *guys* means male or boys," the moment becomes a turning point for literacy learning and learning literacy.

**Principle 8.** *Understands that (a)gender and gender identity transect with other identities (e.g., sexual orientation, culture, language, age, religion, social class, body type, accent, height, ability, disability, and national origin) and informs students' beliefs and, thereby, actions.*

Example 1:

Together, stakeholders and students can participate in dialogue about their collective identities. To the extent possible, they can unpack how their identities are shaped in different contexts, through different communities, through their own and others' beliefs, and through different policies. Building, they can reflect about how their identities impact their actions and inactions. They can consider what might hold them back, or, what motivates them to act. They may reflect on examples where they wish they might have intervened or in which they observed someone else be offended. This discussion should account for the pros and cons of intervening and the possible consequences, i.e., the physical dangers, of stepping up.

Example 2:

Stakeholders can approach pedagogy, curriculum, students, and others through a transectional mindset. Through a sustained approach, stakeholders, students included, can come to understand how shifts in mindsets within these educational contexts will increase capacities for how they approach others in their lived worlds. What can emerge are possibilities for contexts to change and, over time, the impact can generate a deeper understanding of humanity.

**Principle 9.** *Advocates for equity across all expressions of (a)gender and gender identities.*

Example 1:

Stakeholders can openly discuss their beliefs around gender identity injustice by drawing upon examples of prejudice, identity contingencies, and stereotyping. They can advocate that these individuals have the right to express themselves without fear of violence. They can speak with others, develop a robust gender-identity-related vocabulary (see Appendix G), develop a deeper understanding of issues facing their students, insist on professional development at all institutional levels (e.g., state and local superintendents and their cabinets, and school board members), form coalitions and change policy, connect with local community organizations, conduct a gender identity audit of the educational context, and determine how to make and sustain it as a safe and welcoming environment (see Appendix H). Building from these findings, they can create and commit to principles that align with their work environment (see Appendix I).

Example 2:

Stakeholders can reevaluate the physical environment, the advisors, and the naming of their Gay/Straight/Queer and Sexual Diversity Alliances. The titles of these groups impact who attends and who attends affects who doesn't attend. Students of color tend to avoid the alliances because they typically fail to attend to trans-sectional identities, and when the groups are situated in beliefs and values that reflect white power and privilege, it reinforces the cycles of oppression that already structure most educational contexts.

**Principle 10.** *Believes that students who identify on a continuum of gender identities deserve to learn in environments free of bullying and harassment.*

Example 1:

Stakeholders can take an active role in intervening when they see or observe prejudice or violence against students with complex gender identities. To the extent possible, stakeholders should agree to a plan about how to hold each other accountable. This might include on-going professional development, study groups, attending events, resituating and renaming bathrooms and locker rooms, updating all documents and forms, ensuring that gender identity is enumerated in anti-bullying policies, studying Title IX and Title VII and subsequent legal cases that draw on them, watching documentaries (see Appendix J), practicing scenarios (see Appendix K) and working with experts who can offer additional supports and services.

Example 2:

These statements can be read regularly and be pointed to as a constant reminder about the importance of respect for self and others. They may be put into memos, syllabi, codes of conduct, made into posters or placards, and read at events, etc.

### Philosophy Toward Students

This educational context supports, affirms, and recognizes the diverse backgrounds and nature of students with myriad identities. All students are invited to share their continuums of culture, language, age, social class, body type, color, accents, heights, abilities, disabilities, (a)genders, gender expressions or creativities, gender identities, (a)sexual orientations, medical status, political affiliations, religions, spiritual beliefs, creeds, veteran status, language, mental health, immigration status, national origins, health status, and the indeterminate. Honoring your identities underscores not only your own psycho-emotional-cognitive development, but the growth of all your future students...

### Personal Accountability to You and Us to Each Other

Students and faculty each have responsibility for maintaining an appropriate learning environment. Professional courtesy and sensitivity are especially important with respect to individuals and topics associated with continuums of culture, language, age, social class, body type, color, accents, heights, abilities, disabilities, (a)genders, gender expressions or creativities, gender identities, (a)sexual orientations, medical status, political affiliations, religions, spiritual beliefs, creeds, veteran status, language, mental health, immigration status, national origins, health status, and the indeterminate. Class rosters are provided to the instructor with the student's legal name. I will gladly honor your request to address you by your claimed name and (a)gender pronoun. Please advise me of this preference so that I may make appropriate changes to my records.

## Allies in the Struggle for Gender Identity Self-Determination

Being an ally is a privilege; something someone "can" be, but doesn't have to. An alliance one can don and remove at will is not a true ally. People can don hats, jackets, shirts, but true ally-ship is a lifelong commitment to living in solidarity with others. This means standing with and stepping up with others and not waiting until there is an issue for those whose gender identities incur attacks. It means being active and with the work the entire time—it's a life commitment to closely working with others on shifting the conditions that have structured the schooling system that positions certain bodies as vulnerable. It means understanding how logics continue to open different doors for some to access certain privileges while generating mediocre opportunities, at best, for others (Miller, 2018b). The strategies identified here are living the commitment of being an ally in this work. Five additional commitments are then presented for being and living as an ally and shifting conditions and mindsets about gender identity complexity in schooling practices.

- Only give talks or workshops where there are bathrooms in the building that honor ALL lives.
- Attend conferences in cities or states where gender identity is protected and don't where policy makers have made dangerous threats or statements about discriminatory practices targeted at those whose identities are vulnerabilized.
- Divest from relationships and institutional structures (e.g., businesses, companies, places of learning) that reinforce and sustain the marginalization of those who are undervalued, under-mis-or not recognized at all, silenced, queer, have complex gender identities, are non-white, etc. Stand with those who work against this marginalization.
- Live a life that embodies and is committed to eschewing certain privileges, even when you have access to them.

- Stay focused on learning about how (school) systems have and continue to grant power, falsify security, and sustain neo-iterations of change or reform.
- Ask for support from cis and non-cis folks.
- Stay in the know: read, watch the news, turn to social media outlets and online.

## Commitment One: Invest Emotionally in the Well-Being of Students so They Can Exist in Schools Without Fear of Attack for Gender Presentation

For Commitment One, stakeholders can begin by asking, "In what ways are students harmed? What should be changed?" They can then look closely at how codes of conduct, forms, bathrooms, locker rooms, physical education classes, extracurricular participation regulations (especially in sports), school counseling and mental-health services, and language and terminology use attend to the needs of, and reflect, a continuum of gender identities (see Miller, 2015a, 2016 for detailed examples). In all areas noted above, groups can strive to ensure that all students' gender identities will be supported, recognized, and valued in school as well as work to ensure that professional development prepares teachers, administrators, staff, and other school personnel to use language and terminology that reflect a continuum of gender identities. If we begin to reframe gender identity as a mediator for animating learning, we can develop increased capacities for kindness, understanding, and gender identity justice. Planting new roots that attend to topics of gender identity in schooling practices can shift mind-sets and change both practices and policies.

Students can be asked how they want to be called on or referred to. Any professional development must prepare teachers, administrators, and curriculum specialists to include opportunities that mirror or expand awareness and respect regarding a continuum of gender identities. There should be concerted attempts to include texts, films, writing assignments, images, art(ists), media representations, athletes, trailblazers, political movements, histories, musicians, poets, key figures, and others that reflect different representations of gender identities. An ongoing focus group to study the effects these artifacts have on the schooling environment can provide key recommendations for continuing change. Expanding on these efforts, small or large groups might be formed to study a text, an issue, or a policy or to visit a local community organization and fold in strategies that can support gender identity inclusivity in schools.

## Commitment Two: Carve Out Strategies to Address the Inclusion of a Continuum of Gender Identities School-Wide

Commitment Two asks "What kinds of support do stakeholders need to effectively attend to this work." Surveys and interviews can assess what stakeholders know and want to know as well as how to apply knowledge to their contexts. Questions about background knowledge related to gender identity can be used to generate professional development opportunities. Stakeholders can be invited to name experts they would like to learn from; which films, videos, and texts they would like to see or read; and which conferences they would like to attend. Stakeholders can be encouraged to engage in research between pre-K–12 schools and university teacher education programs to better understand the school through students' eyes and build findings into both contexts' curricula.

## Commitment Three: Plan and Map How to Create New Opportunities Where New Social Relations Can Form

For Commitment Three, stakeholders can be asked, "How is power built into the dynamics of gender identity and how do those dynamics need to be shifted?" In surveys, focus groups, professional development, and other settings stakeholders can be asked to reflect on how their own gender identities maintain and sustain gender identity hierarches of power and how they create harm. Opportunities to closely reflect (as a group and individually) on how gender-typical identities maintain and sustain gender identity power dynamics can be offered. Facilitated groups can look into how intersectional identities are maintained through neoliberalism. Based on what emerges, a long-term plan for both how to study those effects and how to shift the schooling environment can be developed. Some possible questions that can lead this process might include, "Do certain students cluster in only some classrooms?" "Is there a Gay Straight, Gender and Sexuality, or Queer and Sexuality Alliance, and who attends those meetings?" "Who doesn't attend those meetings and what can be changed?" "Do we need to rename the club to be more expansive?" "How can we bring students and teachers together so our school is safe for everyone?" Finally, a committee can be formed to put up gender identity expansive posters, signs, billboards, and art throughout the school; to generate recommendations for classroom rearrangements; to ensure that more books with diverse gender identity representations are in classrooms and the library; to invite speakers; to host movies and videos; and to work with others to rename spaces in the school where all gender identities are recognized.

## Commitment Four: Plan and Map How to Shift Power Dynamics Around Allocations of Social Space, Curricula, and Innovations

Commitment Four asks how to navigate this work from the ground up. To this aim, stakeholders can take a group walk through the school to determine what spaces are funded more than others. After, a group can be assembled to examine and create a portfolio about how power operates and is sustained in the school. Based on those findings, resources (money, larger rooms, technology, etc.) can be redistributed so power is shifted for evenness. Pedagogy and curricula can also be assessed to identify if trans-sectionality, (the intersections of trans\*+ bodies with school practices; see Miller, in press) is reflected in school practice. For example, pedagogies that are monologic, authoritative, pedantic, and not culturally relevant and responsive can diminish students' motivations to learn. Based on what is identified, curricula can be changed to ensure that trans-sectional voices are not peripheral, misrecognized, or unnamed and that equity for all is rooted in the classroom. Beyond this, stakeholders can develop whole-school models for assessing ongoing processes related to shifting dynamics of gender identity. For instance, long-term checks and balances can be implemented to continually assess the suggestions in Commitment Four.

Next, the school can work closely with neighboring universities' teacher education programs. This might include discussions about how to embed gender identity work across grade levels and disciplinary areas in preservice teacher education, account for gender identity, develop lesson plans and pedagogy, and/or consider co-created possibilities for research. Last, schools can review if and how spaces at school are liberatory; how spaces reinforce dynamics of power about gender identity; and how and by whom power is held in that space so they can collectively plan how to reframe the space so different gender identities have equal parity.

## Commitment Five: Continually Assess How Changes Are Working and Invite Stakeholders to Help Address and Create Forward-Thinking Solutions

Commitment Five, the final commitment, asks stakeholders to consider how strategies have been effective in exposing or confronting the root causes that maintain an educational gender identity industrial complex (i.e., gender policing) and what needs to be done to build the school (world) they want to live in. Based on the answers, stakeholders can generate a list of reflections that address awareness about root causes of gender identity subjugation. A survey can then be compiled and distributed. Once the findings are collected and analyzed, they can be folded into continued efforts to challenge root causes of gender identity inequities.

Additionally, stakeholders can reflect on what the school environment should look like and then construct a plan for wants and needs that will galvanize its realization. To achieve this, working groups can be formed to identify issues that need improvement and to generate an action plan that will help achieve the desired outcomes. Throughout these efforts, it is important to reflect on whether root approaches to work are trans-sectional. This can be achieved by evaluating how students' trans-secting identities frame the core of discussions. Disaggregating data can help to reveal where disproportionality is situated so changes can be made.

Another strategy is to cultivate new leaders who have the vision to challenge and change the system. For example, schools can create a strategic action plan that addresses the kinds of leadership styles and vested interests that should be manifested in their school and then work to ensure that those styles and interests are present. Then schools can determine strategies for district, school-wide, and individual accountability. Once those strategies are developed, teams can revisit and/or create the mission and vision statements for the district and the schools, develop an equity profile that assesses how these criteria are implemented, demonstrate how to assess changes over time (e.g., by informal, formative, or summative means), and map out how to make changes.

Schools can also develop a statewide network dedicated to working with legislatures who can create and change policies. Schools can create a long-term plan that addresses new policies and changes and organize ongoing discussions and meetings for their schools, related, but not to limited to, sports, enumeration of antibullying laws, dress, bathroom and locker room access, mental-health services, health care, body safety, disciplinary practices (e.g., zero-tolerance policies and overuse of subjective discipline infraction categories), identification rights, and others.

Concluding Commitment Five is the need to assess whether efforts are process-oriented rather than end-oriented. This means striving to ensure that all endeavors reflect a continuum of gender identity inclusivity and the indeterminate for any person's self-identification. It also means staying open and aware to what may still come and remaining open to the work that will continue to support elasticity.

Although the interlocking of beliefs, practices, and policies has somewhat changed to include gender-identity-complexity recognition in schools, cosmetic changes do little to help establish fairer and more equitable schooling environments. These efforts must continue to look into root causes and ways to change the exclusionary political, economic, and affective practices and their subsequent conditions that have created injustice in the first place. Such work should be started before kindergarten so that its impact can be seen, felt, and sustained over time.

For this work to have a transformative effect and ultimately be enduring, it must be built collaboratively from the bottom and requires levels of commitment from various stakeholders, such as ourselves, students, teachers, administrators, staff and school personnel (anyone who has contact with youth), parents, communities, teacher education programs (deans, professors, preservice students), researchers, and policymakers that orbit and work in, for, and on behalf of schools.[13]

## Target Reconsidered: Resetting the Pedagogical Default about Gender Identity

If we were to think back to the scene in Target and consider if these individuals had been conditioned to read the world through a trans-sectional lens, the event may have played out differently altogether. How could, then, a trans-sectional lens become another ingrained lens through which the world can be seen and a way of reading the world? This would not be a dismissal or discarding of other readings of analyses entirely, but it is advocating for a more complex and contextually grounded way, similar to the both/and, to read the world through a braided analysis.

These questions might be used to frame larger discussions about what might have happened in Target had each of the players had these tools. This is then followed by opportunities to consider how you might now approach people in different contexts.

*Target*
- Discuss how each player might have read the context differently in Target.
- Consider how they might have objectively approached the situation.
- Discuss how the scene might have played out. What might the outcome have been?

*You, as you first read the scene*
- Discuss the scene and describe your reading.
- Consider the impact your view might have had on someone else.

*Now that you have read this chapter*
- Discuss how you now read the context in Target.
- Discuss and describe each person.
- Consider the impact this revised view might or could now have.
- What tools would you be comfortable using in this or in a similar situation?
- In what ways will you apply any of the tools in your reading of Target elsewhere?
- How might you share or teach others about some of these tools?

*Other questions to consider*
- What cis privileges were you either aware of unaware of having?
- How have you been positioned based on your gender identity? Was that true about you? If not, how did that feel?
- How have you positioned others based on their gender identities? Do you have a sense of how that might have impacted others?
- What presumptions or assumptions have you made about gender identity?

*Possible outcomes*

In considering how possible outcomes from the analyses of these questions can have long-term impact in educational contexts—any context—it requires a monumental shift. For its impact to transform environments, shifts in mindsets, thinking, and behavior must be rooted in foundational structures, embedded in processes, and applied in practices. These foundations include, but are hardly limited to, educational settings. By applying a trans-sectional lens to discussions about gender identity for those going into higher administration, teacher education, pre-K–12th grade preservice preparation, and student support and services, it can begin to generate a critical mass of awareness that can lead to systemic change. Continuing along this trajectory, it should be threaded into professional development for all stakeholders in schools, and be woven into policies, curricula, and practice in all education-related areas. The work must have movement and it must be sustained over time, especially given "the explicit assimilationist and antidemocratic monolingual/monocultural [monogendered] educational policies emerging ..." (Paris and Alim, 2014, p. 88). Sustaining trans-cultural complex gender identity is vital *and*, starting today, right now, the work must begin in pre-K classrooms and then be reinforced for the remainder of a student's education in *all* contexts related to schooling practices.

Engendering these approaches in contexts, opens up spaces where trans-sectional and ever-evolving, indeterminate gender identities will be understood and recognized to be asset-based, rich sources for learning literacy and literacy learning. When trans-sectionality is recognized as a core lens through which to view students' (all people's) lived experiences and another basis for learning and teaching, schools are building new foundations about understanding, recognizing, and legitimizing (Miller, 2016, 2018a, 2019) gender identity and for potentially changing how gender identity is perceived in society.

By moving away from presumptions that sustain cis-and gender identity normative defaults and resetting and recasting them to and through a trans-sectional gaze, hitting refresh will foreground trans-sections of identities as a new starting point for gender identity work.

As more students self-determine their gender identities it will indeed signal that there is movement toward a state of being trans-culturally sustained. As a team—and this work does require a team—we *can* hit refresh that resets to a default where trans-sectionality becomes a starting point about how to think about gender identities. The more often refresh is hit, the broader the momentum to change educational contexts and the beyond. Such work will shift, change, embed, and sustain linguistic, literate, and cultural pluralism in schooling practices, and can bring about social transformation. As trans-sectionality becomes more rooted in ordinary cognitive processes, it helps put into place new structures to envision how schools can be a source for changing how gender identity is framed in society. Perhaps one day, this lens may become a new default....

## Sustaining Contexts that Embrace Gender Identity Complexities

In order for this work to have broader social impact—for it to be sustained—and for it to be enduring—we each have to all do our inner work. Trans*++ and gender-identity-complex folk have to work on their educative and personal responses to others, and cis-folk need to stay in the work, by living it in concert with their day-to-day lives. None of us has all of the answers, but—and sorry to employ a cliché—but change, and transformation, can ultimately be part of the ordinary existence, where cis and non-cis folk interact without fear, concern, or anxiety. While current work may seem to be making only small visible differences, everything we do in the here and now, and what has transpired before that, has galvanized change and recognition, is critical to long-term and sustained changes. Every effort we put into the here and now is creating a world for those coming in and exiting, and a hope is that one day, the complexities of gender identity will no longer be an "issue" or a "problem" that needs to be addressed; that it will be an ordinary aspect of the day-to-day lives of everyone and people will not be forced to tolerate misrecognition or feign indifference in order to thwart harm. If we cannot have these public debates and are left to only have them in private spaces, then how can make necessary changes happen? We need to move these private discussions in to the daily interactions so we can disrupt and interrupt moments, in order to consider strategies that can leverage and expand on our skills as we navigate different contexts. If not at the gas station, then where? If not the bank, then where? If not school then where: And, of course, if not Target, then....

In the day-to-day of our lives—whether it be those annoying errands, sitting through meetings that could have been handled in an email, stopping for gas, even taking a walk down the street, or shopping at Target—if these seemingly mundane routines were part of a broader human network in terms of how they are experienced and read, the cutting incident may have played out quite differently. Regardless of someone's height, clothing styles and colors, hair color and styles, type of shoes, mannerisms, gestures, behaviors, or silences, our understanding and applying of a trans-sectional lens of others can be a rich source that both advocates for and expands how people can work through concerns and fears about communicating and messaging about gender identity complexities. And, yes even in/on line at Target.

We can never truly know another's story: we can only know our own (if we're lucky). Withholding presumptions and assumptions about others does require self-monitoring and personal critique. As we hold ourselves accountable to these efforts, we will develop new cognitive and behavioral skills that, over time, as practiced and trained, will become muscles. But, muscles cannot be left alone or they will flatten; like muscles, then, this work requires on-going training, care, and rest, which can lead to increased capacities for creating spaces for people to self-determine their gender identities. With a growing mass of increased awareness, society becomes more humane, understanding, and welcoming, and while scenes in Target will likely still occur, the impact may be diminished, short lived, and less debilitating.

# Notes

1     **Trans**˙⁺, which is technically synonymous with, though etymologically different from, trans*, trans*⁺, and transgender, is the experience of having a gender identity that is different from one's biological sex. A transgender person *may* identify with the opposite biological gender or identify outside of the binary altogether. A trans*⁺ person may or may not be pre-or post-operative and is not defined by an essentialized gender formula. This term has become an umbrella term for nonconforming gender identity and expression.

Trans*⁺ when written with an asterisk and superscript plus sign, denotes transgender identities that continue to emerge as indeterminate. Trans* with only an asterisk denotes a segment of the transgender population that is inclusive of only some trans people's identities, while excluding others. In my writing, I use the superscript plus sign *⁺ to symbolize the ever-expanding and indeterminate ways of self-identifying, and the asterisk to honor those who fought for gender identity self-determination and paved way for new identities to emerge.

Trans is a prefix or adjective used as an abbreviation of transgender, derived from the Greek word meaning "across from" or "on the other side of." Many consider trans to be an inclusive and useful umbrella term. When the prefix is affixed to gender it signifies all non-cisgender gender identities and a recognition of difference from cisgender people.

2     **Gender identity self-determination** is the state of, and right to, self-identify in a way that authenticates one's self-expression and self-acceptance, and which refuses to be externally controlled, defined, or regulated.

3     **Gender identity complexity** is the constant integration of new ideas and concepts and the invention of new knowledges—comprised of multitudes, and/or, a moving away, or sometimes a refusal to accept essentialized constructions of binaries, genders, and bodies. Yet, in simultaneity, gender identity can be some of these, all of these, and none of these. It avoids the straightjacket of being categorized. Also written as *complex gender identity/identities, gender identity complex* or the *complexity/ complexities of gender identity/identities*.

4   **Cisgender/cis or cissexual** denotes a person who by nature or by choice
    conforms to gender-based expectations of society. Cisgender individuals
    have a gender identity that tends to be aligned with their birth sex,
    and thereby tend to have a self-perception and gender expression that
    matches behaviors and roles considered appropriate for their birth sex.
    Cisgender people are also on a continuum of gender identities and
    there is no one way that a cisgender person *must* be. It is important to
    recognize that even if two people identify as men (one being cis and
    the other being trans*⁺⁺), they may lead very similar lives but deal with
    different struggles pertaining to their birth sex. The prefix cis is of Latin
    origin, meaning "on the same side (as)" and evolved from the use of the
    term transgender as a recognition and signifier that there are different
    types of gender identities.

5   Different combinations of responses—or not—are contextual and can
    be inventive, culturally specific, descriptive, or prescriptive. Responses
    constantly change and shift over time as they transect with new ideas,
    experiences, and contexts.

6   Some people say in line, others say on line so I combined them.

7   Use of they, them, their, theirs, or themselves will be used as third person
    singular identifiers instead of gender-specific pronouns.

8   This section has been modified and reprinted from Miller, 2019.

9   This is also originally The Queer Literacy Framework: A queer literacy
    framework promoting (a)gender and self-determination and justice.
    Modified but originally printed. (Copyright 2015 by the National Council
    of Teachers of English. Reprinted with permission.)

10  The GICF can be modified for other identities and for different cultural
    and linguistic populations.

11  The use of the word "current" signifies that gender identity and naming
    are on a continuum and demonstrates the awareness that it can shift
    depending on time, context, and circumstances.

12  While it is prescriptive and perceived as culturally correct that American
    English uses the third person singular pronouns he/him/his and she/her/
    hers to signify how speakers name genders, we have recently seen the
    entrance into our lexicon (even at the great outrage of prescriptivists)
    of *they*, in both use and usage in the *AP Stylebook*. The *AP Stylebook*
    shows the singular "they" and its derivative forms, them/their/theirs, or
    themselves as demarcation of a wide range of gender identities. This shift

marks a movement away from the presumption of how one self-identifies and moves us into a gender-neutral state. A main rationale for this move was that when a pronoun is selected for one's identity, it marked it as sexist. Because many of us, by no fault of our own, have been conditioned to write (and speak) using male and female pronouns, this gendered lexical indexing provides an opportunity for us to further engage in the work.

13 The commitments have been reprinted from Miller, 2018b.

# 3

# Critical Consumption of Transgender and Nonbinary Representations in Popular Culture and Social Media

Rhea Ashley Hoskin, Jessie Earl, and Ashleigh Yule

In Thomas King's (2003) book *The Truth About Stories*, the Indigenous scholar describes the relationship between storytelling and experience. Stories, King argues, not only shape who we are but how we relate to and interact with each other. The stories we tell are important; they can be hopeful, inspiring, and validating—but they can also be alienating, and create division among people. Storytelling is a fundamental aspect of our world: from creation stories and religion, to social media, politics, popular culture, film, television, books, plays, and music. Each medium tells a story and, in telling a story, reproduces particular sets of norms, relations, and ideologies. If popular culture is a primary means of storytelling for the masses, what does this mean for people who have been historically relegated to the outskirts of dominant narratives? For example, what do the stories we tell mean for transgender and non-binary (TGNB) folks, and what relationships are we cultivating in the stories told by popular culture? This chapter explores some of the stories that have been told about TGNB people, beginning with an overview of how TGNB identities have been conflated, then moving into a micro-analysis of gender codes and how popular culture's use of gender codes instills transphobia. We will then explore contemporary TGNB narratives, themes, and issues, including an examination of what we call community-driven representation: social media produced by TGNB people. Finally, the chapter concludes by discussing the importance of visibility and good representation in promoting TGNB resilience.

## Dominant Discourse: Conflation and (Mis) Representation

Talking about TGNB representation requires a broadly cast net, one that spans across literature, medical textbooks, comic books, anime/manga, video games, theatre, YouTube and other social media platforms, not to mention film and television, as well as one that includes the broader cisgender LGB community, drag queens—even cisgender heterosexuals! In other words, trans representation cannot be distilled to the representation of TGNB within dominant popular cultural media alone, but must also consider dominant cultural uses of gender and, more specifically, how cisnormativity and transphobia are discursively produced using these outlets. This holistic view of how gender has been understood and adopted— across media as well as identities— makes up the current and historical ideologies that contribute to TGNB representation.

The early years of popular culture were marked by sexual science, wherein sexologists like Havelock Ellis (1859–1939) wrongfully concluded "homosexuality"[1] to be sexual inversion. To this end, Ellis (1927) theorized that "homosexuals" experience incongruence between physical sex and internal sense of gender. In other words, rather than focusing on the subject of sexual desire, sexologists interpreted same-sex sexuality as an expression of gender identity—that lesbians wanted to be men, and gay men wanted to be women. Of course, we now know this is not the case,[2] and that such notions of gender inversion are deeply couched in heteronormativity and constricted conceptualizations of binary gender. Indeed, we are now better equipped with a variety of terms to describe a plethora of beautifully complex identities, embodiments, and expressions, and are much more adept at discerning sex and gender identity from sexual orientation.[3] Unfortunately, the medical industrial complex has maintained a steady hold on gendered ideals; constructions which are, in turn, discursively produced and maintained via popular culture (Hoskin, 2018b). Through popular culture, gender norms are disseminated and bodies are regulated in ways that maintain white, cisgender, able-bodied heterosexual men as the norm. Considering this relationship, it's not surprising that sexologists' conflation of sex, gender, and sexuality via the theory of sexual inversion appeared within mass media and dominant knowledge.

Sexologists' interpretations seem to have had a lasting, trickle-down effect on popular culture, such that most early depictions of trans folks were conflated or homogenized under the "gay umbrella." So, while this book is about TGNB experiences, the early years of trans representation meant the conflation between gender identity or expression, and sexual desire. Thus, it becomes necessary to discuss LGBTQ+ identities more broadly as an initial stepping stone in order to talk more directly to contemporary representation of TGNB folks.

Looking at popular cultural representations around the turn of the century showcases how dominant culture struggled to grapple with the ideas of sex, gender, and sexuality. In fact, other than depictions of their murders or the added shock value of the "trans reveal," TGNB people were largely absent, homogenized, or "indirectly" represented via proxy-characters. The director of *Love, Simon*, Greg Berlanti, described these types of representations as doing "math in your head of switching the genders of characters to get through it psychologically ..." (Bell, 2018). Proxy-representations, which we're using to describe depictions of gender in ways that contributed to dominant ideologies of trans identities and transgender representations, were both useful and harmful. Sometimes proxy-representations mimic queer baiting; tip-toeing around the idea or representation of gender diversity, but never explicitly naming it. While queer baiting is typically intentional, proxy-representation comes from creators using stereotypical characteristics of LGBTQ+ identities without understanding the implications. On the one hand, some proxy-representations have proven to be extremely harmful and uphold cissexism, such as with *Silence of the Lambs* serial killer Buffalo Bill being given transgender characteristics to accentuate their insanity. On the other hand, proxy-representations can be positive, allowing for queer-readings of cultural texts that allow trans folks to "see" themselves in dominant culture.

One excellent example that encapsulates the confusion between gender and sexuality allowing for positive transgender proxy-representation comes from a 1992 episode of *Star Trek: The Next Generation* titled "The Outcast." In this particular episode, the writers of *Star Trek*, a franchise long known for its willingness to tackle social issues of the day through science fiction allegory, hoped to tackle the persecution of homosexuality within western cultures but ended up with a fairly progressive proxy-representation of TGNB folks. In "The Outcast," the male series regular Commander Riker falls in love with Soren, a member of an agender (i.e., having no gender) alien species known as the J'naii. Soren reveals to Riker that she actually identifies as a woman, which goes against the social norms of her society. J'naii society "corrects" these "aberrations" by forcing citizens to undergo psychotectic therapy, which maintains an agender norm. When Soren and Riker's relationship is revealed, Soren is put on trial. Despite a rousing speech, Soren's pleas are ignored, ultimately leading to her "correction" and a heart-broken Riker.

While the episode is far from perfect, particularly in its damaging representation of asexual and agender people as cold and aloof, it showcases how the confusion between sexual orientation and gender identity as well as proxy-representations can ultimately be positive. The writers never intended a TGNB analogy; they thought that creating aliens with a non-binary gender identity was simply a "clever" science fiction concept that would never exist in the real world (surprise, it does!). As a result, while the writers intended the story to represent allegorical sexual-orientation persecution, it instead reads as literal transgender persecution. The episode even discusses issues of pronoun use, binary gender roles, gendered gatekeeping, and many other still-pertinent topics within gender and trans conversations. Yet regardless of the episode's faults and its main mistake of conflating gender and sexuality, TGNB viewers were able to find representation through a character that was never intended to actually represent them. The audience is meant to sympathize with Soren, who expresses her identity articulately and stands up for herself. Many viewers have found Soren to be one of the earliest positive proxy-representations of TGNB people in mainstream science fiction.

Proxy-representations can also be found within the history of LGBTQ+ representation, where TGNB identities have been subsumed under various terms or identities. For example, trans has a long history of being conflated with crossdressing and drag. However, trans folks also share a legitimate, yet tumultuous, history with many of these subsumed identities. Additionally, while it is commonly known now that drag and trans are not the same and that it is both inaccurate and highly offensive to conflate the two, many trans folks have commented on how drag allowed them to connect with their authentic selves. For example, *RuPaul's Drag Race* season 9 contestant Peppermint, a transgender woman, noted that drag allowed her to see a part of herself not previously depicted in popular culture, and gave her permission to experiment with gender. These types of representation, while flawed, allowed for trans people to carve a space within popular culture wherein they could see themselves.

Despite this complex shared history, mainstream drag mogul RuPaul in particular and the *Drag Race* enterprise in general have faced warranted criticism for exclusionary practices and opinions regarding having transwomen compete on Drag Race.[4] RuPaul commented:

> Drag loses its sense of danger and its sense of irony once it's not men doing it, because at its core it's a social statement and a big f-you to male-dominated culture. So, for men to do it, it's really punk rock, because it's a real rejection of masculinity. (Aikenhead, 2018).

This comment sparked much debate within the LGBTQ+ community over transphobia in the *Drag Race* series. When asked whether women would be allowed to partake in the competition, particularly with respect to Peppermint, RuPaul stated, "[i]t's an interesting area. Peppermint didn't get breast implants until after she left the show; she was identifying as a woman, but she hadn't really transitioned" (Aikenhead, 2018).

Here, RuPaul has inserted himself into a longstanding debate over who or what is a woman—thank you, Simone de Beauvoir (1989)! How do we qualify womanhood, and what makes a woman, well … a woman? Is it her hormonal profile? Research led by Anne Fausto-Sterling (1992; 2012), Sari van Anders (2017) and Janet Hyde et al. (2019) has shown how hormones span a continuum in a not-so-discreetly-dichotomous sort of way. Plus, hormones change over time, and are reactive to the social world. So, hormones can't define who is and is not a woman. Is it how a woman is treated by a patriarchal society? Is one somehow more a woman if she experiences more sexism? This seems to be a fairly reductionist view of womanhood. Perhaps menstruation is how women ought to be qualified? Does that mean that post-menopausal women are disqualified? What about cisgender women with amenorrhea, or transgender men and non-binary people who bleed? Maybe what truly makes a woman is her breasts, as RuPaul seems to suggest? Well, women have varying sizes of breast, and some do not have breasts at all! Plus, it seems pretty sexist to reduce a woman to her breasts—not very in line with RuPaul's big "F you" to the patriarchy! But we digress. As we scratch away all the qualifiers of woman, we are left with only one: self-identification. Yet, RuPaul's comment upholds the idea that trans folks who have undergone surgery are somehow more authentic than those who have not (or could not) and attempts to add another curious qualifier to the womanhood checklist. A gender-qualifying checklist certainly seems at odds with the goals of drag.

At its core, drag is a form of art that interrogates gender—but the performance itself is not necessarily a reflection of how the performer identifies. By gatekeeping who is allowed to partake in the competition, *RuPaul's Drag Race* polices both art and trans bodies. What has historically been a queer art performed in a safe space, and used to challenge cisheteropatriarchy has been weaponized in the hands of mass media and reformed into an exclusionary tool used to enforce binary gender and sex. If you're shaking your heads at how hypocritical that seems, we're with you.

What's more, drag has always been an integral, though separate, part of the trans community and vice versa. To deny that history, that leading role, seems a violent form of erasure. Take, for instance, Sylvia Rivera or Marsha P. Johnson, whom many would consider the mothers of the Trans Rights movements. Both Rivera and Johnson self-identified as drag queens, despite showcasing and articulating identities that we would qualify as transgender today. Human categories are majestically blurry, messy, and complex, aren't they?

Some have argued that this erasure is a consequence of the mainstreaming of drag—crafting a respectable, normative drag queen who does not confuse the binary order of gender/sex but, rather, jumps the fence from time to time to put on a good show! To align drag with trans runs the risk of politicization and the subsequent failure to cultivate a consumable mainstream image of drag. In other words, opening the door to the politicization of drag runs the risk of drag no longer being palatable for a wider audience (read: straight and cisgender). Such an egregious notion is assimilationist at its core and stands in opposition to LGBTQ+ movements—pride in who we are, not in who dominant culture would like us to be.

## Learning Code: Instilling Associative and Ideological Transphobia

The early years of trans representation were dismal: problematic, conflated, reductive, or non-existent. These subpar representations were damaging and continue to fuel contemporary cisnormativity through proxy-representations that reduce cross-gender coding to the brunt of jokes, a costume, and effectively associate trans people as deceptive (Hoskin, 2019; Bettcher, 2006, 2013; Serano, 2007). Take, for instance, the proxy-representation prevalent in '90s comedy, whereby cisgender men essentially perform drag—what we call the "man in a dress trope." Notably, this trope has a long history in the acting world dating back to Shakespearean times, when female characters were performed by prepubescent male actors because having women perform on stage was considered socially unacceptable at the time. Today, this schtick, performed by cisgender male actors, upholds that a presumably male person dressed in "women's clothing" is inherently laughable. A plethora of actors have adopted cross-gender codes as a comedic device, such as Robin Williams in *Mrs. Doubtfire*, Eddie Murphy's Fat Mama in *The Nutty Professor*, Tyler Perry's character of Mabel "Madea" Simmons, Martin Lawrence in *Big Momma's House*, and Jack Lemmon and Tony Curtis in *Some Like It Hot*. Of course, none of these characters are trans. However, we must pay attention to how gender, particularly cross-gender coding, perpetuates particular ideologies that can be harmful to trans persons. Recent scholarship emerging from Critical Femininities highlights how femininity is frequently made the brunt of a joke or a punch line, pegging this tired comedic strategy on the cultural tendency to view femininity as an artifice, a performance, or otherwise inauthentic (Hoskin 2017; Hoskin 2018a; Serano 2007). Ultimately this strategy lends itself to the tendency to view femininity, and those who are perceived to be feminine, as somehow deceptive. In addition to reducing femininity in men to a punch line, the man in a dress trope also discursively produces the idea that "genders that cross" might also be deceptive, or have ulterior motive, as was the case for Dustin Hoffman in *Tootsie* where he poses as a woman to attract more jobs.

Importantly, while popular-culture consumers may roar with delight at the sight of a man in a dress whether on stage or on screen, they would likely recoil to sit next to the exact same gender configuration/ embodiment on the subway (Butler, 1988). Perhaps the great joy and pleasure western society derives from mocking femininity speaks to what psychoanalysts call the "fear of the feminine" (Kierski and Blazina, 2009), where the "feminine joke" becomes a tool to disarm feminine power (Hoskin, 2019; hooks, 1992). While the stage or the screen allow for separation between the viewer and performer that maintains femininity as an artifice, the same gender expression in daily life, existing independently and as a self-governed expression, calls the fragile order of normative sex/gender/sexual systems into question.

Other forms of proxy-representation seemingly pushed some sexist boundaries and brought a critical gaze to gender performance, such as Amanda Bynes in *She's the Man*—a modern-day retelling of Shakespeare's *Twelfth Night*. Yet, these gender-crossing portrayals still upheld the belief that, underneath it all, there is still a biologically determined sex that is the "true" identity, which does little other than perpetuate inaccurate notions of sex/gender and harm TGNB people. What's more, these representations uphold gender-crossing as being about something—anything—other than based in one's true identity. Why else would a cisgender boy or man dress like a woman if not some sort of a ruse to undermine a custody ruling and secretly spend time with his children (e.g., *Mrs. Doubtfire*) or to infiltrate a girls' soccer team as a "secret weapon" (e.g., *Lady Bugs*). From a very young age, children are indoctrinated with gender norms, and the way popular culture attends to "gender transgression" is no exception. Even Bugs Bunny, who crossdressed in order to trick Elmer Fudd, played a role instilling a future generation to believe that gender transgressions are mere trickery or for the purpose of disguise.

In addition to portraying gender transgression as "disguise" with an ulterior motive, they have also been used as a plot device whereby the audience is made aware and the plot revolves around when or if the character will be revealed for who or what they truly are; for example, Marlon and Shawn Wayans in *White Chicks* or Nathan Lane in *The Bird Cage*. These representations hold up an essentialist notion of identity by symbolically attaching trans identities to a costume or something "put on" while reproducing biologically assigned sex as more valid, natural, or authentic.

Consumers of popular culture need to engage critically with these texts, unpack the messages that are sent via cross-gender coding, and understand how these codes are used to further particular plots. What is the ultimate message that is attached to a character's use of gender? It is disconcerting to consider the message of gender-transgression-as-deception alongside a second theme within the early years of representation: gender-variance as evil (i.e., villains). It comes without surprise that by subtly reproducing gender-transgression as deception, a next logical step is the association of gender-transgression as "evil." In particular, children's content tends to signal that someone is a villain, or to craft a villainous persona, by using subtle cross-gender codes. For example, Disney has a history of continuously reproducing subtle gender-transgressions as signifying the antagonist—otherwise known as "queer coding." Queer coding assigns stereotypical queer traits to characters, such as flamboyancy, femininity, talking with a lisp, being prim, wanton, or vain (Jagose, 1996). These "codes" are used symbolically as a sign of immorality. For example, Disney characters such as Jaffar in *Aladdin*; Ursula in *The Little Mermaid*, whose character was inspired by drag queens; Haiti in *Hercules*; Radcliff from *Pocahontas*; Scar from *The Lion King*; or Tamatoa the treasure-hoarding coconut crab in *Moana* have all used queer codes (i.e., non-normative gender codes) in order to craft an evil, immoral persona.

These depictions use varying degrees of subtlety to instill the lesson to be distrustful of those who transgress gender norms. Sometimes these are explicit. Such is the case for *Ace Ventura: Pet Detective* when Ace discovers that Lt. Lois Einhorn is a trans woman—or, as the film frames it, that Lt. Lois Einhorn and Ray Finkle are the same person. In the scenes immediately following Ace's realization, he repeatedly exclaims, "Einhorn is a man!" as a sour, disgusted expression becomes increasingly prominent on his face. Ace is then shown hurling in the toilet, dramatically brushing his teeth, burning his clothes, and crying in the shower (in a scene that almost draws parallels to depictions of sexual assault), all while Boy George's "The Crying Game" plays in the background. In the subsequent scene where Ace "exposes" Einhorn in front of the police squad, he points a gun at her head while repeatedly calling her a liar. Questioning Einhorn's authenticity as a woman, Ace violently pulls her hair, rips off her shirt to expose her breasts, tears off her pants to reveal her penis to an assembled audience, all while continuously misgendering her. The scene ends where Ace's realization began: the police force puking in the corner while "The Crying Game" plays in the background. This scene not only upholds previous tropes such as trans people having an agenda or ulterior motive, as being deceptive, or as being villainous, it also inscribes a message that trans people are disgusting.

Unfortunately, Ace Ventura isn't an anomaly, and the trope of trans femininity as nefarious—or even sociopathic—is fairly routine. Similar films like *Silence of the Lambs*, James McAvoy's Patricia in *Split*, and Norman Bates in *Psycho*, all use trans coding in ways that ultimately instill in the audience that trans folks are creepy and weird. Even Tim Curry's portrayal of a "sweet transvestite from Transylvania" in the cult classic *Rocky Horror Picture Show* contributes a questionable proxy-representation. The film's 2016 remake drew attention to the popularity of the proxy-representation when it cast famous transgender actress Laverne Cox in Curry's original role. Yet, both the original and the modern adaptation use trans coding to set an "eerie" scene of human experimentation and innocence lost, a scene so aptly described in the 1992 film *The Crying Game* as a world "where nothing is at it seems to be."

Day-time talk show hosts Jerry Springer and Maury Povich routinely played into this trope, hosting countless episodes that revolved around the "surprise" reveal of someone's trans status. While the '90s audience seemed endlessly fascinated by the "reveal" narrative, these episodes ultimately portrayed trans folks as duping their unsuspecting romantic interests. Additionally, this fascination was underscored by the tendency of dominant culture to hold cisgender as natural, "normal," and unremarkable, which further sensationalized trans bodies.

At this point we anticipate our readers may pause to think—"wait, for the most part these representations are proxy-trans feminine." You are correct! This pattern is symptomatic of something bigger happening in dominant culture and LGBTQ+ communities at large: trans misogyny and femmephobia. While trans femininity is coded as the brunt of joke, deceptive, and immoral, proxy-trans masculinity (or the ways that we learn about masculine codes) paint a somewhat different picture. Take, for instance, Joan of Arc, Eponine in *Les Miserables*, or Disney's *Mulan*, each of whom crossdresses in order to fight alongside men. While still coding gender transgression as having an ulterior motive, masculinity remains coded as a social promotion.

## The Monstrous and the Mundane: Absented Proxy-Trans Masculinities

The focus on proxy-trans feminine representations nevertheless begs the question of why there is such a dearth of trans masculine—or even proxy-trans masculine—representations in popular culture. Two lines of thought could be used to explain this discrepancy: the monstrous and the mundane. At the time that Jack Halberstam wrote *Female Masculinity* (1998), masculinity expressed by those assigned female at birth was seen and categorized as ugly and monstrous. In response, one of the goals of Halberstam's book was to rescue "female masculinity" from the monstrosity to which it had been assigned in the public eye. Thus, a first and perhaps initial explanation for the lack of proxy-trans masculine representation relates back to the omnipresent male gaze (Mulvey, 1975). Because "ugly women," as they had so been classified, did not participate in patriarchal beauty norms or appeal to the male gaze, perhaps they were seen as needing to be hidden from public view and thus did not garner attention from popular culture.

A second hypothesis is that proxy-trans masculinity is mundane or unremarkable, which can be explained through Serrano's (2007) concept of effemimania. Effemimania refers to the stigmatization of "male" expressions of femininity or entrances into the "feminine realm," as well as the cultural preoccupation with "male femininity" more broadly. According to Serano (2007), there is no equivalent phenomenon for "female" expressions of masculinity or entrances into the "masculine realm." Serano explains that this phenomenon is caused by the hegemonic hierarchical placing of masculinity above femininity, whereby the policing of femininity is allowable. This is echoed within psychosocial and clinical literature, which finds trans femininity to be more heavily policed and regulated than trans masculinity (e.g., Susset, 2014; HRC, 2018; see Hoskin, 2017 for an overview). In other words, gender norm violations are not met with the same volatility for individuals who were assigned female at birth who present masculine. This can be seen clearly in the social repercussions for tomboys versus "sissies" (Susset, 2014). In a patriarchal society, perhaps it makes sense that someone assigned female would want to be a man, but to want to be a woman is considered pathological (Serano, 2007). Effemimania thus affords a certain "shock value" that makes transfeminine proxy representations highly consumable to a cisgender audience. In general, femininity tends to be objectified, and is seen as performative, or as spectacle. This is exemplified by the qualitative difference in popularity between drag queens and kings, with drag queen culture being much more widespread and admired than that of drag kings. Perhaps this is because drag kings elicit a certain discomfort that creates disinterest? Or perhaps masculinity is not seen as something that can be performed because it stands as gender neutral (Hoskin, 2018a). To suggest otherwise would be to challenge patriarchal power.

As a result, masculinity may be seen as a promotion, and thus may have become almost mundane, essentially erasing opportunities for proxy-trans masculine representations. For example, it is common to see women wearing pants, with short hair, or coded in other ways that might be considered masculine. Typically, these representations are either "mundane" or they are a social promotion as noted in the above examples (Hoskin, 2013). Thus, masculinity for those AFAB (assigned female at birth) is more normalized and seen as less remarkable than someone AMAB (assigned male at birth) who is feminine, which adds a highly consumable "shock value" or comedic device to any given plot.

## A Tragic Life, A Cautionary Tale: Popular Culture as a Disciplinary Force

At the same time, while subtle cues have been used to imply or explicitly depict trans folks as villains or deceivers, they were simultaneously portrayed as victims —in these early years of representation, it was almost an "either/or" situation. Arguably, this polarity can be explained as the latter (i.e., deception) justifying the former (i.e., murder). In other words, taken together these two tropes act as a legitimizing discourse for hate crimes observable within the dominant media —that murder of trans people is somehow legitimized by their assumed deception, and the subsequent "panic" reaction of the perpetrator. Consumers of pop culture must develop a critical lens when it comes to gender codes, particularly narratives that suggest trans folks as deceivers. Whether through subtle cues or overt plot, these narratives function as a later justification for trans victimization. The "rhetoric of deception" has a long and continued history (e.g., Christine Jorgensen), one that rears its head in the news, particularly in relation to trans violence (Bettcher, 2006). Bettcher (2006) argues that such representations of trans people as deceptive and inauthentic operate as a tactic to both justify and promote violence against trans people. Shows like *Law & Order: Special Victims Unit* routinely depicted trans sex-workers as victims of rape, violence, and murder. These depictions create a particular scheme within the minds of both cis and trans consumers, one that gives ideological permission for violence against trans folks, and the other that paints a dismal future for trans folks.

To quote a punk-rock girl from East Berlin who dreamed of life on the other side of the wall, "but how to get over? People died trying" (*Hedwig and the Angry Inch*, 2001). Trans folks, like queer folks in general, yearn for the other side, to see a future after transitioning, and/or coming-out. Instead, to borrow from Foucault (1978) and necropolitics (Mbembe, 2003), whether by suicide or murder, trans representation created a dominant message that trans people were "made for dead," and that such a fate has been deemed consumable by mass media. Ultimately, when taken together, these messages serve as cautionary tales for young or emerging TGNB people; a tale that is echoed in the rates at which trans folks are murdered or die by suicide. At the same time that popular culture is conditioning and teaching the masses to associate gender transgressions as evil, deceptive, and a joke, these messages are also being consumed by trans youth. It is troubling to dissect the cissexist and transmisogynistic codes that are taught through popular culture; it is even more troubling to consider how they are internalized by trans youth. Not only did early representations cause undue confusion over sex, sexuality, and gender as a result of their conflation, it also deeply ingrained the cultural message that something is wrong with trans people.

This message has also been conveyed through the censorship and subsequent erasure of TGNB folks in shows like the Japanese series *Sailor Moon* (Hoskin, 2016). In the original series, *Sailor Moon* offered a plethora of progressive queer and TGNB characters: Amara, Zoisite, Fisheye, and the Sailor Starlights. In the original series Fisheye, whom an American audience might understand as non-binary or a trans woman, is described as a "miraculous person that surpasses genders." Yet this scene is dubbed and effectively cis-washed for an American audience to instead say, "you're beautiful and have a unique look." The erasure of Fisheye in the '90s carried symbolic meaning that continues to weigh heavily on the shoulders of trans folks today. By erasing or only representing trans subjecthood in death, as a joke, or as deceptive, many of the early representations failed to open up cognitive space for trans existence but, rather, shut down possibilities and hope.

## Cisgender Gaze: A Compassionate Contradiction?

As we turn to look at more contemporary pop culture representation, we begin to see a shift toward compassionate, positive portrayals of transgender and non-binary identities. While the issues of the past still find their way into the zeitgeist, such as in films like 2011's *The Hangover Part 2* and 2017's *Zoolander 2*, as well TV shows like *It's Always Sunny in Philadelphia*, *South Park*, and, most recently, Amazon's *Jack Ryan*, the overarching trend of transgender narratives have shown a shift toward the sympathetic. However, even these depictions of transgender life bring with them their own assumptions, shortcomings, and pitfalls. These pitfalls of modern portrayals of transgender identity can best be described through the lens of a "cisgender gaze," an idea that derives its meaning from the concept of the "male gaze." Arising out of feminist film theory, the "male gaze" refers to how in literature and the visual arts, women are presented as sexual objects that exist for the consumption by, and pleasure of, men. Women are reduced to objects of fascination, something to be looked at and enjoyed but never given agency (Mulvey, 1975). As a consequence, women come to internalize this omnipresent male gaze and begin to evaluate themselves through men's eyes.

The male gaze takes a variety forms and has far-reaching impacts, such as how and where women are allowed to have agency in narratives. A simplified view of the male gaze can best be exemplified by a film audience being given a male point-of-view in order to center a male narrative, typically at the expense of women. Think of how we are introduced to Megan Fox's character in director Michael Bay's 2007 film *Transformers*: a camera shot from Shia LaBeouf's point-of-view as Fox sexily bends over a car engine with her midriff exposed, back arched, and breasts prominently framed. Bay gives power to LaBeouf's male character, forcing the audience to identify with his character and see the female character as something external.

Through a male gaze, women come to be seen as an "Other," separate from the "normality" of manhood. Masculinity is made to feel natural and dominant, whereas femininity becomes contrived and passive. In the same way, visual media and literature normalizes masculinity, so too does popular culture center a cisgender experience at the cost of "Othering" transgender experiences. Through a cisgender gaze, transgender lives become spectacle, something to ogle at or scrutinize by virtue of how different they are from an "everyday" cisgender lifestyle. For example, popular culture tends to focus on how a transgender experience directly differentiates from a cisgender experience. This is what Bauer and colleagues (2009) refer to as cisnormativity; "the expectation that all people are cissexual, that those assigned male at birth always grow up to be men and those assigned female at birth always grow up to be women" (p. 356). By discursively reproducing cisgender as the norm, popular cultural representations shape social attitudes toward TGNB people, and the ways in which TGNB individuals navigate their social landscapes. In addition, as modern understanding and cultural sympathy has grown for transgender people, the cis gaze has resulted in transgender representation falling into two major narratives—transition and oppression.[5]

## The Transition Narrative

The transition narrative focuses on how transgender lives first visually deviate from cisgender lives. Cinema is a visual medium that thrives on the power of juxtaposition. As a result, a fascination with the purported visual distinctions of a trans and cis experience follows as a natural step in transgender representation. The audience is presented with a visual device to distinguish trans people from cis; trans people are presented as looking inherently different from a cisgender person by having sex characteristics typically culturally assigned to two different genders – a trans woman with soft skin and breasts but an Adam's apple or sharper jaw, or a trans man with facial stubble and flat chest but wider hips or shorter stature.

Yet, this visual juxtaposition is also mirrored by the film's structure. Most films typically begin with a status quo familiar to the assumed audience, which is, in most cases, assumed to be cisgender. Transition narratives typically begin with a transgender character living as most cisgender people do—in accordance with their gender assigned at birth. Yet, as the film progresses, the audience follows the trans character as they move further from a "normal" cis experience to that of a trans person living as the "opposite" gender. The use of hormones, surgical interventions, and changes in gender expression all become plot points on the road from a cisgender to a transgender life.

A transition narrative also focuses on the internal juxtaposition within the trans character themself. We see the character struggle with the decision to change their gender. As the film progresses, this struggle changes to how they navigate moving from understanding their one gender experience to another. The character ultimately finds resolution when they fully accept their new gender, having made a complete move from one pole to the other.

A clear example of a transition narrative is the 2015 film *The Danish Girl*, which received an Oscar for Eddie Redmayne's portrayal of real-life trans woman Lili Elbe living in 1920s Copenhagen. The film starts with Lili living as a man with her loving and supportive wife. As the story continues, we see Lili push further from her "cisgender lifestyle." We follow her through each step; dressing in women's clothing, dating men, leaving her wife, and ultimately undergoing a series of surgeries. All the while, the audience gazes upon Lili's internal struggle as she learns "how best" to be a woman. Before dying from complications due to surgery, Lili comes to terms with living as woman full-time with zero qualms with her identity, the polar opposite of how she began the film. Where earlier audiences reveled in the "trans reveal" narrative, contemporary audiences delighted in media that highlights the "transition narrative," as depicted in *Transparent, Degrassi, Becoming Chaz, Becoming Julia, This is Everything, I Am Jazz,* and *I Am Cait.*

The transition narrative requires the juxtaposition of moving from one binary gender to another. Consequently, this narrative not only reinforces a binary notion of gender, but it also functions to erase non-binary identities from the purview of popular culture. The spectacle of transition works better and is more palatable for a mass, presumably cisgender, audience when a trans character moves discreetly between two binary extremes, such as man to woman or woman to man, rather than to something that, at least visually, appears to be in the middle of the two. However, there are a few examples of non-binary representation that challenge the transition narrative, such as the Sailor Starlights in *Sailor Moon*. In their Earth bodies, the Sailor Starlights are intelligible as masculine men. When they transform into their superhero form, the audience watches as the Starlights' bodies re-shape and their embodiment turns feminine. The Starlights move between and across binary understandings of gender, and demonstrate how gender expression can be contextual and ever-shifting (Hoskin, 2016). Recent representations also include Yael in the Canadian series *Degrassi: Next Class*, or Susie[6] in *The Chilling Adventures of Sabrina*. While both characters do not fit the binary-transition model, they do uphold another reductive representation: that non-binary identities are limited to white-passing, androgynous/masculine-of-center folks who were assigned female at birth. In general, non-binary representation is sparse, but the visibility of non-binary people of color who are femme or assigned male at birth is all but nonexistent.

## The Oppression Narrative

The oppression narrative focuses less on the individual distinction between cisgender and transgender experiences and more on the societal differences between the two. These stories focus on how transgender people are subjected to transphobia, homophobia, misogyny, and bigotry; the audience follows a trans person as they must fight against the injustices that society throws at them. Transgender people are put on a pedestal, presented as elegant human beings who fight to have "normal" lives while facing adversity. By the end of the narrative, the trans person successfully combats and overcomes the oppression, such as in 2017's *A Fantastic Woman*, or fails to defeat the injustice resulting in punishment, such as with Laverne Cox's incarcerated character in *Orange is the New Black*, or dies, like Jared Leto's trans woman character in *Dallas Buyers Club*. Other examples of this narrative can be found in *Anything, A Kid Like Jake, 3 Generations, Boys Don't Cry, The Orville* and even as far back as aforementioned *Star Trek: The Next Generation* episode "The Outcast"; an episode title that itself exemplifies the oppression narrative.

Transition and oppression narratives also differ in how they position cisnormativity. In the transition narrative, the differences between cis and trans are represented within the film itself through a character that moves from a "normal" cisgender experience to an "abnormal" transgender one. However, oppression narratives juxtapose a transgender experience against the film audience's assumed cisgender experience. The film asks the assumed cisgender audience to watch how a transgender character's life is radically different from their own. This implicit assumption is underscored by the perspective taken within films; one that piques a cisgender curiosity by centering a plot on its insight into an "unknown" existence, or an existence fundamentally different from that of a cisgender person. Within this framework, cisgender people are assumed to find entertainment watching a trans person struggle against the daily oppression that cisgender people typically do not face on a regular basis.

## Impacts of Cisgender Gaze and Transition/Oppression Narratives

Both oppression and transition narratives use the cisgender gaze to portray transgender characters sympathetically. Yet, in both narratives, the audience is asked to pity the transgender character, rather than to genuinely empathize with them. Transgender characters are not portrayed as being included within cultural constructions of "Us." Rather, TGNB people are an out-group who are perpetually kept at the peripheries and for whom dominant culture should certainly feel badly. The resultant Us/Them divide upholds the idea that TGNB people do not have existences akin to cisgender folks, or that trans people are wholly defined by their trans-status. In each of these stories, a character's defining characteristic is that they are transgender. It is the first and most prominent fact that the audience knows about them. After watching these films, it is unlikely the viewer could recall a single characteristic about TGNB characters before stating they are transgender. Transpeople become "fantastic," as the title of *A Fantastic Woman* states, simply by the nature of who they are.

The cisgender gaze also intersects with a male gaze to produce particular representations. First, as an audience is assumed to be male, straight, *and* cisgender, most representations of trans people are transgender women or proxy-trans feminine. Second, these characters are symptomatic of the Madonna/whore dichotomy that systematically divides women as being pure, saintly, and deserving of respect, or slutty, impure, and undeserving of human dignity (Bordo, 1993). Trans people are either loved and respected (a "Madonna") or desired and reviled (a "whore"). "Madonna" trans people are typically older, upper-class, white women (e.g., Maura Pfefferman from *Transparent* or the cultural fascination with Caitlyn Jenner). "Whore" trans people are typically younger, lower class, women sex workers who are typically people of color, such as in *CSI: Crime Scene Investigation*, *Pose*, or *Tangerine*.

## "Transface"

In recent years, the concept of "transface"[7] has become a pressing issue (Reynolds, 2015). Analogous to the concept of "blackface," where white vaudeville and film performers would use makeup in order to portray black people as racist stereotypes, transface refers to the casting of cisgender actors to play transgender characters (Earl, 2018). A particularly troubling outcome of transface is the reinforcement of biodeterministic views of gender. For example, transgender women are typically played by cisgender men and transmen by cis gender women, which enforces biodeterminism, or the idea that one's biological sex determines gender. Transface says that underneath the makeup, transwomen are still men, and that transmen are still women under the suit.

As sympathy for transgender issues has become more mainstream, Hollywood tends to continually pat itself on the back for showcase transgender narratives. Transgender portrayal in *The Crying Game, The Danish Girl, Boys Don't Cry*, and *Dallas Buyers Club* have all resulted in Oscar nominations and wins for cisgender actors, as well as Emmy wins for cisgender actors or creators for TV shows like *Transparent* and *Orange is the New Black*. Yet, with rare exceptions, these award-winning projects do not include actual transgender involvement whether on-screen, creatively, educationally, or financially. In essence, cisgender actors and other creatives further their own careers on the back of transgender disenfranchisement. Their awards and accolades re-enforce a cisgender-only economy, while simultaneously appropriating transgender stories.

Unfortunately, trans people's attempt to challenge transface or a cisgender gaze is often shut down by the expectation that they be grateful for any representation whatsoever. The right to complain is revoked from trans people under the guise of creative freedom. For example, many cisgender artists, actors, directors, or other creatives argue that anyone should be allowed to play any character. When renowned cisgender and LGBTQ+-supportive actress Cate Blanchett was asked about the issue of cross-identity roles, she stated, "I will fight to the death for the right to suspend disbelief and play roles beyond my experience" (Voss, 2018). While these arguments do have artistic merit, they are ignorant of the damage that these narratives cause by their implications of transgender life. Such perspectives also ignore that transgender people are rarely given the chance to contribute to their own stories or to participate within the domain of popular culture. By contrast, transgender actors and creatives are rarely hired for projects, and are typically only considered for trans roles, which ultimately go to cisgender people because a trans actor lacks "star power." Issues of "star power" put trans actors in a double-bind: not hired due to a lack of success and unable to *achieve* said success because they are not hired.

## Beyond the Cisgender Gaze: Normalizing Transgender Narratives

While the analyses thus far have been critical of dominant narratives, it is important to recognize that these stories have also had positive outcomes for the transgender community. Popular cultural portrayals of trans people have been crucial in increasing awareness of transgender issues and initiating conversations within the mainstream. While there is still a lot of progress to be made—in terms of representation and other arenas—perhaps we would not have advanced in terms of transgender inclusion without popular media's shift toward a sympathetic view of transgender life.

Indeed, the past few years have witnessed significant growth in terms of popular media moving beyond a cisgender gaze. Content is increasingly showcasing transgender people living everyday lives, normalizing their experiences alongside their cisgender counterparts. In these narratives, a transgender character's gender identity is not inconsequential, but it is not the focus. Additionally, these representations usually feature transgender actors playing trans characters as well as transgender (or at least queer) creatives behind the camera.

For example, in the Netflix series *Sense8*, we meet Nomi, a hacker and notorious feminist blogger who shares a consciousness with seven cisgender characters. Nomi's transgender identity is central within a few of her storylines, such as her relationship with her parents, or informing how she relates to other characters (e.g., she empathizes with a gay man through their shared queer identities). Yet, she also has numerous storylines and relationships that don't focus on her being transgender and is defined more by her abilities as a hacker than by her transness. Additionally, the Wachowski Sisters, the transgender directors of *The Matrix,* created *Sense8* and expressed a commitment to ensuring trans representation behind the camera as well as on screen.

There are several other notable examples that also shift toward normalizing transgender experiences. *Pose* is a TV series focusing on 1980s New York ball culture and features over fifty transgender characters, all played by transgender actors. *Pose* also centers transgender creators such as director/producer Janet Mock and writer/producer Our Lady J. The Arrowverse, a DC-Comics-superhero-shared universe of TV shows, gave us numerous LGBTQ+ characters, including the world's first live-action transgender superhero on *Supergirl*, played by transgender advocate and actor Nicole Maines. *Assassination Nation* stars transgender model Hari Nef in a female revenge film that satirizes the mob-mentality that colors our current political, social, and gender discourse. The TV show *Billions* showcases non-binary actor Asia Kate Dillon as a non-binary character thriving in the world of finance.

However, while these portrayals do not define their trans characters by their transness within the shows themselves, it perhaps is still telling that the characters' transness is still their defining feature in the marketing of the content to a real-world audience. Additionally, there is often a scene within the shows themselves where the transgender character must explain their transgender identity to other characters, otherwise the audience may not understand them simply by watching their stories unfold.

## Financial Influences and Other Markets

To date, there have yet to be normalized portrayals of transgender lives in big-budget Hollywood films. As financial investors are less willing to take risks on larger-budget productions, normalized representations emerge from lower-budget, niche, and often science fiction TV series. Given that the very existence of transgender identities remains heavily politicized, inserting transgender characters in big-budget productions sadly carries the assumption of an "agenda," which upholds the belief that TGNB storylines pose a financial risk. Additionally, Hollywood has grown more reliant on the burgeoning Chinese film market, both in production and distribution. As China still has anti-LGBTQ+ policies that limit film distribution to the country, and thus a larger amount of profit, studios have tended to ignore transgender storylines.

While the mass market has lagged in terms of transgender inclusion, other media with more niche markets and less financial pressure have been a haven for diverse transgender representation. Successful comic books like *Saga, Bitch Planet,* and *Batgirl* have all featured well-received transgender characters. Novels like *Dreadnaught* and the fantasy series *Broken Earth*, which was the first series to win the science fiction literature Hugo Award three years in a row, also includes trans characters. Additionally, while video games have grown into a gargantuan industry over the past few decades, their audience has primarily focused on the *generally* more accepting millennial and younger audience of the United States, Western European, and Japanese markets (Earnest, 2018). Consequently, this allows the representation of transgender identities to carry a lesser assumption of financial risk. Best-selling games like *Dragon Age, Night in the Woods* and *Assassin's Creed* have featured transgender characters and *South Park: The Fractured But Whole*, a media franchise known for problematic portrayals of trans people, surprisingly became one of the first video games to allow a player to choose if their avatar is transgender or cisgender, after selecting a binary gender identity.

While there appears to be a trend towards better portrayal of transgender people, it is still worth noting that these representations still tend to be binary-identified white transgender women. There is still a dearth of trans men, non-binary people, and transgender people of color. When trans people of color are portrayed, they are typically lower-class, sex workers, or criminals, such as in *Tangerine, Pose,* or *Orange is the New Black.* Arguably, this problematic and limited representation can be traced to the increased consumability or mainstreaming of white feminism, which centers the oppression of white women over the oppression of other, more vulnerable groups.

Yet, with the growth of social media and creator-focused distribution platforms like YouTube, mixed with the lowering cost of production brought on by the digital era, transgender-community-made content has exploded all across the internet. This type of content does not filter through a studio, film festival, video game publisher, comic book publisher, or other form of distribution network, but instead gets released to the public directly from the creator themselves. Examples include the Emmy-winning web series *Her Story*, documentary series such as Laura Jane Grace's *True Trans*, webcomics like *Assigned Male, Up and Out,* and *Trans Boy Diaries*, as well as transgender-focused or inclusive podcasts like *The Gender Rebels, Bit Different, The Advocates, LGBTQ&A, Queery,* and *Nancy.*

## Community-Driven Content and Social Media Influencers

The largest and perhaps most popular version of community-driven content comes from individual YouTube personalities. Like much of the content on the platform, TGNB content on YouTube often comes in the form of individual "influencers," those who have gained a large social media following because of their content.

The most successful influencers like Gigi Gorgeous and Jazz Jennings tend to be those who cultivate a larger audience. Often such "star power" is cultivated by catering to the cisgender gaze and is typically in the form of vlogs (video blogs) discussing issues of fashion, hormones, or surgery. Both Jazz and Gigi have had success outside of their YouTube by following this formula (e.g., Jazz has a book and TV show, and Gigi has a wide-release documentary). Additionally, both are binary-identified trans women, the identities centered by a cisgender gaze. This is by no means a condemnation of their content. Instead, it showcases how their content speaks to the larger social narrative of transgender people, thus creating more financial viability to these creators. Through their work and their visibility, both Gigi and Jazz have helped improve the conversation around transgender topics.

Other successful influencers focus on educational content and to educate their viewers about transgender issues—creating vlogs and videos about trans topics, as well as how they may intersect with issues of gender, sexuality, race, politics, social justice, or a variety of topics. Popular YouTubers like Ash Hardell, Kat Blaque, Riley J. Dennis, Jackson Bird, Chase Ross, Skylar Kergil, and Jessie Gender (a contributing author to this chapter) have all created content that breaks down complicated topics into easily digestible videos (e.g., the gender spectrum, transface, and pop culture representation of trans people). These videos typically use humor and anecdotal stories to help viewers identify with the seemingly "unrelatable" topics.

The photography/short-form video-based social media platform Instagram also features a large section of transgender influencers. As Instagram tends to attract even younger audiences than Facebook and YouTube, these representations of trans life predominantly impact transgender youth who are looking for role models or visual representations of a transgender journey. Instagram representations also follow similar patterns as their YouTube counterparts. Some influencers such as Hunter Klugkist, Emerson Palmer, and *Biff and I* focus on transition-related content, giving hope to many transgender youth who try to learn what a transition may look like. Some influencers attempt to normalize trans experiences, depicting trans people going about a daily life without the transition or oppression narratives put forth by dominant pop culture. In particular, Instagrammers like Justin Blake, Miles McKenna, and London Pidel bolster this type of content. Finally, as Instagram is a mainly visual platform, there are many influencers who work to provide visual inspiration for transgender identities (e.g., modeling, bodybuilding, fitness, and diversity of appearance and abilities). They reassure the viewer that trans bodies are beautiful whether they fit into a white ableist cisnormative heteropatriarchal beauty standard, or break free from it. Influencers such as Broxton Walker, Christopher Rhodes, and Aydian Dowling attempt to run counter to a cisnormative ideal of what you must look like or what body parts you must have in order to appear beautiful.

Many social media influencers also release other forms of content, such as Ash Hardell's (2016) *ABCs of LGBT+*, an amazing book that uses color graphics, personal stories, and humor to help explain the seemingly endless amount of sexualities, genders, and identities within the queer community (and is a great book to give anyone, queer or not, who is looking for an easy-to-read introduction to LGBTQ+ communities). Additionally, social media influencers diverge from popular culture in a particularly important way. While popular culture tends to focus on white, straight, cisgender upper-middle-class men, social media influencers tend to come from a larger variety of identities across the spectrums of race, sexuality, sex, gender, abilities, gender expression, and social class. Influencers also have a much more direct relationship with their audience; often building a community through Twitter, Facebook, YouTube, or Instagram and allowing their audience to directly fund their videos through crowd-funding sites like Patreon. Perhaps at the crux of community-driven content, audiences are often given the opportunity to suggest the topics of an influencer's content through social media. Combined with the rapid frequency of their content (typically weekly releases as compared to the monthly or yearly wait between other forms of media), community-driven representation not only enables the audience to feel like they are building a much more personal relationship with the content and the creators behind that content, but to also see themselves reflected in their surrounding world.

## Representation Matters: Visibility and Resiliency

It is clear that the landscape of transgender representation is rapidly changing and building momentum across platforms. But why does this matter? The real-world implications of better trans representation are reflected in the academic literature across disciplines, including education, public health, critical theory, psychology, policy development, and others. It is paramount that trends in representation be examined alongside risk, resiliency, and the overall well-being of TGNB individuals. Indeed, understanding representation and visibility is not only of chief importance for transgender individuals, but is also essential in order for non-transgender family members, educators, and service providers to establish and maintain best practices for transgender and gender-diverse youth in all areas of their lives.

### Resilience Among Transgender and Non-Binary People

While it is clear that TGNB people experience multiple and significant risks (see Appendix L for an overview), recent research has also identified that TGNB youth possess incredible tenacity, strength, and competence (Veale et al., 2015; Stieglitz, 2010; Travers et al., 2012). Indeed, many transgender and gender-diverse youth move into healthy and successful adulthoods despite the significant hurdles they face throughout their lives (Simons, Liebowitz, and Hidalgo, 2014; Wells et al., 2017). Though resilience factors are not often as focal in the clinical narrative about transgender youth, we know that family acceptance and support; competent, gender affirming professional and medical care; safe and supportive schools; gender- and sexual-diversity-inclusive curricula and policies; peer and community support; and student clubs contribute to positive outcomes for trans and gender-diverse youth (Bauer et al., 2015; Simons, Schrager, Clark, Belzer, and Olson, 2013; Toomey, Ryan, Diaz, Card, and Russell, 2010; Veale et al., 2015; Wells et al., 2017). Arguably, many of these sources of support are developed through education, dismantling biodeterministic gender, and community, each of which can be fostered through visibility and *good* representation. Strengths-based research clearly indicates that representation, visibility, and community are essential components of resilience for trans youth (Erhensaft, 2016; Murchison, 2016), whereas erasure, lack of representation, and poor representation often exacerbate risk factors within the trans community (e.g., Hatzenbuehler et al., 2014; Hatzenbuehler, McLaughlin, Keyes, and Hasin, 2010, Hendricks and Testa, 2012). As such, both the evolution and the future of trans representation are important to consider related to the health and well-being of transgender and gender diverse youth.

## Erasure, Lack of Representation, and Poor Representation

Despite important areas of progress and awareness, most youth still grow up in a heteronormative, cisnormative social context in which sexual and gender diversity are absent or are poorly represented. Indeed, many transgender and gender-diverse youth report that they were not aware that others also experienced discomfort with their assigned sex, or that "being trans" or gender diverse was "a thing." Many TGNB individuals disclose being the only TGNB person they knew growing up, being told that their gender diversity was a problem to be fixed, or thinking that they were the only trans person in their school, town, city, province, state, or country (Veale et al., 2015).

The historical lack of visibility of transgender characters, experiences, and identities in media contributes directly to the inaccurate and harmful ideas that trans people do not exist, or exist only very rarely and tragically. Further, as previously noted, when trans stories did appear in books, movies, TV shows, and other media, one-dimensional characterizations and fetishization often further reinforced the isolating message that transgender people were unusual, singular, and mentally ill. Such inaccurate and essentialized messaging further perpetuates harmful stereotypes and inaccuracies about trans people, which directly escalates the isolation and alone-ness many trans youth experience in their families, schools, and communities.

The negative mental health impacts of such erasure, lack of representation, and poor representation cannot be understated. As one trans youth from one of the authors' practices stated anonymously, "I literally thought I had to be the only transgender person in my entire city. I had no way of knowing that people like me existed, let alone could transition, be happy, or live normal lives" (eighteen-year-old transgender youth). Such experiences may exacerbate the risk factors faced by transgender and gender-diverse youth and contribute to feelings of social isolation and other-ness (Veale et al., 2015).

## Impacts of Visibility and Good Representation.

Advocates within the transgender community as well as trans-health researchers, clinicians, educators, and policymakers have clearly identified that trans visibility matters. Indeed, strengths-based support recommendations for TGNB and gender-diverse youth include accurate, positive depictions of transgender characters, storylines, and experiences (Wells et al., 2017). Such recommendations owe largely to the known positive impacts of shared experience, community, and representation (Veale et al. 2015; Travers et al., 2012). When we can *see* ourselves, *our* experiences, *our* realities reflected in a show we are watching, a book we are reading, a videogame we enjoy playing, or a song on our playlist, it can contribute to reducing feelings of isolation, loneliness, and rejection. This phenomenon has been well documented related to ethno-cultural, racial, and gender minority groups (Dank,

1971), and holds true for sexual and gender minority groups as well (Hendricks and Testa, 2012; Meyer, 2003).

Accurate, everyday representations of trans and gender-diverse experiences also serve to provide non-trans individuals with positive exposure to wider and more diverse portrayals of social groups and individuals. This has been shown to reduce discriminatory attitudes, decrease rigid stereotyping, and enhance social understanding and expressions of empathy (Veale et al., 2015). Such representations can also be helpful for parents, caregivers, educators, and wider society in de-mystifying and normalizing the existence and authenticity of transgender people and experiences. Given the grave risk factors facing transgender and gender-diverse youth, including discrimination, violence, and significant mental health challenges, the potential for representation and visibility of trans stories in media must not be underestimated. Indeed, as identified by many advocates in the trans community, "visibility and representation can be a matter of life and death" (de Sousa, 2018).

# Conclusion

"The truth about stories is that that's all we are"—just a series of interconnected stories that calcify to create personal narratives, interpersonal dynamics, and histories (King, 2003, p. 2). Yet, while popular culture is a powerful means of both storytelling and teaching the masses, it is often trivialized, dismissed, and left unexamined. From the micro-analysis of cross-gender codes, to the overarching patterns observed within representation and how these can be mirrored within clinical literature, it is clear that representation matters. Not only do the narratives and proxy-representations instill cisnormativity and transphobia, they also shape understandings of gender diversity, place limits on the scope of human expression, and inform social relationships. While we have dissected some of the tropes perpetuated through popular culture, we have also illuminated social media as playing an integral role in the cultivation and dissemination of diverse, authentic representations. According to Foucault (1978), where there is power there is resistance. Resistance from the margins causes the minute shifts and adjustments necessary to elicit broader change and to begin reshaping the ruling power. This power shift can be observed in community-driven representation and social media: breaking away from the constraints of white, able-bodied, cisgender hetero-normalcy to instead showcase a multitude of human experiences. Accurate, celebratory, high-quality trans representation in media has the capacity to give voice and representation across intersecting TGNB identities. What an important means to offer hope to the trans youth of tomorrow, to enable them to finally look out into the changing world around them and truly *see* themselves.

# Notes

1    The term "homosexuality" has a history of pathologization and is considered derogatory by many.

2    Although a transgender woman could be a lesbian, just as she could just as easily be bisexual, queer, straight, or any other sexual orientation!

3    For a fun activity, see Sari van Ander's Sexual Configurations Theory and learn how to map and disentangle your own multifaceted identity. https://www.queensu.ca/psychology/van-anders-lab/SCTzine.pdf.

4    While historically there have been many problematic elements of *Drag Race*, especially in terms of transphobic language, it is important to note that RuPaul himself is a queer, black, gender non-conforming older man. Indeed, both RuPaul and *Drag Race* provide a platform for increased visibility of queer and gender diverse people of color within a broader cultural context that makes both gender conformity and whiteness central. Such representation, while flawed, should be acknowledged in discussions of problematic elements of both RuPaul and *Drag Race*.

5    Since the writing of this chapter, the film *Girl* was released and has received widespread criticism from the transgender community. Critics have called the film, which was directed by and stars cisgender

men, "trans trauma porn." The film is indeed grotesque in its gaze of transgender women, ending with the film's protagonist cutting off her penis due to dysphoria. This film is worth noting in this discussion because it is arguably one of the best contemporary examples of the cisgender gaze; particularly the cisgender gaze's influence on transition and oppression narratives.

6   This character was previously known as Susie and used they/them pronouns but, since the writing of this chapter, has changed to the name Theo and the pronouns he/him. Although other characters and viewers alike may be aware of Theo's previous name and pronouns, he is now referred to only by his chosen name and pronouns. This is an important aspect of good representation, as many trans and gender diverse people choose not to have their given/assigned names (also known as "deadnames") known or used in daily life.

7   The term transface is not intended to equate transphobia with racism, or to appropriate blackface; although it certainly runs such a risk. As this point warrants far more critical attention than can be given in the current chapter, we encourage the reader to think through these nuances, how these concepts may be similar, as well as how drawing this parallel can be problematic.

4

# Advocacy Beyond: Continuing Commitments, Personal and Social Growth

Jamison Green

There is a difference between self-advocacy and being an advocate for a cause, whether or not that cause has a personal impact on one's daily life. Ideally, everyone should be their own advocate, but many people are shy about speaking up for themselves. But when one's very existence relies on the capacity of society to grow and change in order to make space for difference, as it sometimes can for trans*⁺ and gender-nonbinary people, the value and necessity of advocacy and activism rapidly becomes apparent.

For many, the term "activist" conjures up images of people who are yelling, often angry, carrying signs and banners, marching in the streets or obstructing traffic, or disrupting the course of daily business. However, significant and effective activism often takes place in very different settings. Activism is the work of changing awareness that is constantly taking place in a wide variety of contexts, despite blatant attempts to marginalize or debase those activities.

For people with trans*⁺ and nonbinary gender identities, activism and self-advocacy frequently happen simultaneously, even when people don't intend to engage in either activity. It was never my intention to be an activist, but when people could not tell whether I was a boy or a girl, and they would confront me about it, I became an activist no matter how I responded to their questions. I was both asserting and defending myself and I was speaking up for an entire class of people (whom I did not know existed, at first) whose gender expression brought them into conflict with the mainstream interpretation of gender, including the assumption that there were—or are—only two genders, and the failure to conform to one or the other—to masculine or feminine—was an indication of failure as a human being. Sometimes people would decide that it was their responsibility, or their duty, or their special opportunity to punish me for my obvious failure of conformity. Sometimes they would express anger with me, sometimes glee, sometimes disgust, sometimes moral superiority. They were always out of bounds. Like the man who, when I was eighteen and at university, tried to kiss and then to rape me because he realized that my body was female. He said I would like it, that God planned it this way, and I should obey God. I had to push him until he tripped and fell, and then I had to run until he gave up chasing me. I was terrified. That was self-advocacy, self-preservation. But on another occasion when I spoke up upon seeing something similar happening to someone else (clearly a man hounding a resistant woman, not someone who was of indeterminate gender expression), when I said out loud, so that others could hear me and judge the situation for themselves, "Stop! You have no right to treat another person that way!"—that was activism.

Activism is work for a cause beyond your own self-interest, though it is frequently inspired or informed by personal experience. When some people speak of activism with disdain, it is because they want to disempower the passion and the drive that activists possess. Advocacy is perceived as much more genteel, more refined. Advocacy usually fits within an established structural mechanism, such as judicial proceedings, or legislative hearings, or committee meetings, where a forum is established to hear the issues. Activism, on the other hand can be unruly, an eruption of frustration or anger, a fervent protest, a leaderless rebellion. Activism is portrayed as much more frightening. And the characterizations of both advocacy and activism are grounded in a power structure that does not appreciate challenges to its authority, a structure that insists on winning. Advocates can find ways to fit within that power structure and to challenge it from within. Some people are capable of being activists and advocates simultaneously, able to work within a system and change rules, policies, procedures, laws, attitudes, and behaviors. Some activists become activists because they have no power, and they must raise their voices to be heard. Their rebellions are chaotic because the people in them are hurt, wounded, damaged, and they have no choice but to cry out. However, whether you are drawn to activism or advocacy, do not let power structures intimidate you into behaving in ways you may regret or that actually set back your cause. Change is not made by inaction. And no one accomplishes systemic change singlehandedly. *Every* cause, if it is to succeed, requires allies.

## Find a Need and Fill It

There is an old adage that speaks to economic success: Find a need and fill it. In other words, if you can discern a need experienced by enough people and establish a way to meet that need that is affordable for all parties in the equation, you will have a profitable enterprise. Making political strides from a position of disempowerment works the same way. This is how trans*+ and gender-nonbinary people were able to make political gains in the late twentieth century and more recently. By volunteering in political campaigns and then in the offices of winning candidates, trans*+ and gender-nonbinary people were able to establish relationships with and build understanding among the people that would ultimately be able to help create laws, policies, and programs that would improve the lives of trans*+ and gender-nonbinary people across the country.

Effective educational efforts aren't as simple to accomplish as realizing that cisgender people need to know that they have privilege and coming up with a training program that tells cisgender people about their privilege in hopes of sensitizing them to the needs of trans*+ and gender-nonbinary people. That's a great solution for those who know they are missing something, and are willing to seek knowledge, but it is not an effective systemic approach. Left to their own devices, many cisgender people are not aware that they have a need to understand people who are not like them. When they don't recognize the need, they have no desire to fill the void, even though their lack of awareness may be stunningly obvious to others.

In the case of the transgender activists volunteering in the offices of politicians, the need they were filling was only indirectly the need for informed politicians; the immediate need at the time was to have clear access to policymakers. Elected officials always need volunteers upon whom they can rely. By making themselves available to fill the politicians' need for volunteers, by being reliable and productive, and by offering themselves as living examples of openly transgender people, these activists made themselves into trusted advisors who could explain community-based issues to the politicians, introduce them to other trans\*\+ and nonbinary community members, and increase the politicians' influence across a variety of political intersections.

Is it possible or even desirable for trans\*\+ and nonbinary people to provide all the education, all the advocacy / activism needed for culture change? I am convinced that trans\*\+ and gender-nonbinary people can't do it all alone. We need allies! Allies bring a variety of strengths and capacities to any group's ability to reach goals. When a group is seeking allies, they would be wise to consider their own weaknesses, and try to cultivate allies who will be able to fill those gaps. Conversely, if one is seeking to become an ally to others, one should consider what is needed in order to be useful. For example, if the group has a great graphic artist but a need for fundraising, and has no one with successful fundraising experience, the members might consider offering to exchange graphic design assistance with an allied group that knows how to successfully approach funders, develop grant proposals, or deliver effective verbal messages that might be enhanced by dynamic visuals. It's a symbiotic relationship that benefits both parties. The strongest allies are the ones who understand and support each other's goals.

One of the most effective ally positions that cisgender people can take is to simply acknowledge the existence and the integrity of trans\*\+ and nonbinary people in every social context. Here are some examples of ways to manifest allyship:

- When trans*⁺ and nonbinary people are not part of the decision-making process, identify the gap and advocate as best you can, including being willing to say, "I don't know about that, we need to get more information from trans*⁺ and nonbinary communities to make sure this makes sense."
- Speak up when others debase or deride trans*⁺ and nonbinary people. Role model respectful, inclusive language.
- Calmly and assuredly dispel any mythology or ridicule that you witness.
- Always make a sincere effort to use requested names and pronouns. Role model acknowledgment and respect. If you make a mistake, simply apologize directly and move on.
- Politely correct others if they use incorrect pronouns or names in reference to trans*⁺ and nonbinary people you know.
- Don't ask about other people's bodies or medical situations.
- Don't discuss the gender status of others unless specifically given permission to do so; don't engage in gossip about trans*⁺ or nonbinary people.
- Wherever you have position power or the ability to assert influence, use your capacity to educate and inform about gender diversity as you support the human rights of all people.

Sometimes an intervention can be as simple as asking a question: "Why do you say that?"

Just trying as gently as possible to understand what another person's position is (or where it comes from) when they say something offensive can be disarming enough to enable them to listen to your perspective, once they've had an opportunity to express theirs, and sometimes they may even admit they didn't realize how offensive or harmful their original words or actions were. These teachable moments are rarely achieved through confrontation. Confrontation almost always results in increased defensiveness or hostility, which is the epitome of closed-mindedness.

In earlier chapters in this book, you will have read about contexts and historical perspectives about trans*⁺ and nonbinary people and their experience. Given what you know now, think about how you might have responded as an ally had you witnessed the incidents described? Could you have made a difference?

## Slow and Steady Wins the Race

There is no controlling the evolution of society. Disruption is possible, and it's something people without power do resort to, but disruption cannot result in any reliably predictable outcome, which makes it a poor strategy. Disruption only produces chaos: chaos cannot achieve a new order without collateral damage, and the extent of those damages is not predictable. Disruption is a tempting tactic, especially when people are frustrated, angry, and full of energy needing direction. Disruptive actions feed a lot of impulses, but they can also play into the hands of the opposition, which, when it is in power, often lies in wait for the "rebels" to expend their limited resources in poorly-planned bursts.

Trans*⁺ and nonbinary people have been struggling to educate the people around them forever. Being more visible and learning to use the media and has helped. There have been many efforts to create educational vehicles that can accomplish feats of more with less—getting the educational points across to more people with less effort. But the nature of gender diversity and the extent of misinformation has rendered such efforts less effective than has been hoped. That doesn't mean anyone should stop trying to do more and better education; it only means that we shouldn't be discouraged. Often people don't learn something until the topic touches them personally. Since relatively few cisgender people are faced with having to think about their own gender, it means that making that personal connection has always been a challenge.

Letting people know that not everyone experiences their gender in the same way is not always easy. Trans*⁺ and nonbinary people who have accepting families and friends may still be reluctant to discuss their situation with strangers, especially when the threat of hostility or violence looms. Many people will laugh, or turn away, or argue, or even become violent when confronted with ideas that challenge their beliefs. But we must persist in building upon the existing knowledge base so that we can all become better at explaining gender to the cisgender masses, leading to safer and healthier lives for trans*+ and nonbinary people.

## We Are Not Alone!

There are many advocacy movement groups around the country, and more will come, so consider these suggestions as a starting point to help you identify additional or more locally accessible groups that share your concerns, or that are advocating on the issues that mean the most to you.

The National Center for Transgender Equality (NCTE) (www. transequality.org) is probably the most effective, professional, and comprehensively focused organization addressing trans*+ and gender-nonbinary issues in the US. The NCTE is based in Washington, DC, and addresses mostly federal policy issues. In the US, federal issues are often played out in state and local government policies as well, so it is wise to keep abreast of what NCTE is blogging about. The NCTE also works to assist state and local organizations working on trans*+ and nonbinary issues.

The Transgender Law Center (TLC) (www.transgenderlawcenter. org) began as a project of the National Center for Lesbian Rights in San Francisco, CA, with grants that limited its scope of activities to the state of California. Once the organization received its own 501(c)(3) status, and expanded its funding sources and its mission, the group began collaborating with groups from other states, and with NCTE. They also moved their headquarters to Oakland, CA, eventually opened a second office in Atlanta, GA. They actively seek volunteers as well as consultants for various grant-funded projects and have a few attorneys on staff. TLC works on a variety of policy issues related to healthcare, jail and prison conditions, workplace issues, and impact litigation.

Impact litigation is the practice of bringing cases to court that have the potential of ultimately effecting social change by reinforcing statutory or constitutional legal principles and spreading the ideas behind them (Harvard Law School, n.d.). Not every legal case, no matter how deeply a litigant might feel about the merits of their case, will have this capacity. Many of the LGBTQ non-profit legal organizations specialize in these types of cases. This type of litigation has been very effective in achieving victories for desegregation, same-sex marriage, and other social issues. The cases that attorneys believe can be used in this way, to create victories for more people than just the immediate litigants, are very few. This can be frustrating for trans*+ and nonbinary people who are suffering because of legal problems and often have difficulties finding attorneys to represent them, either because they have no money to pay for representation, or because there are no attorneys available with enough knowledge of trans*+ and nonbinary experience to adequately provide successful representation. Organizations like The National Center for Lesbian Rights (www.nclrights.org), Lambda Legal (www.lambdalegal.org), GLBTQ Legal Advocates and Defenders (www.glad.org), the Sylvia Rivera Law Project (www.srlp.org), the Transgender Legal Defense and Education Project (www.tldef.org) and the Southern Poverty Law Center (www.splcenter.org) all have done effective trans*+ and nonbinary work and provide educational resources to collaborating advocates and activists. All these groups have special projects focused on youth issues. And these groups, as well as the American Civil Liberties Union (www.aclu.org) all collaborate with the World Professional Association for Transgender Health; GLMA: Health Professionals Advancing LGBTQ Equality; and the advocacy arms of the American Medical Association, American Psychiatric Association, and American Psychological Association, to marshal the latest gender scientific and social science research in service of the values of free expression, autonomy, integrity, and health, including trans-specific health.

Nearly every state in the US has an Equality Federation affiliate. The Equality Federation "is the movement builder and strategic partner to state-based organizations advocating for LGBTQ people. From Equality Florida to Freedom Oklahoma to Basic Rights Oregon, we amplify the power of the state-based LGBTQ movement." (Equality Federation, n.d.). Depending on the type of issues you are working with in your local or statewide situation, you may be able to find support and encouragement through many of these organizations.

As I write this, we are two years into the current four-year presidential term of Donald J. Trump, a man who is guided by conservative religious evangelical Christian control over his party's voter base. Many conservative evangelical Christians (and some members of other fundamentalist religious sects) view trans*+ and nonbinary people as threats to their own faiths and to what they perceive, and their religious texts or leaders define, as the "natural order." (For an objective survey on the subject, see Smith, 2017; see also Johnston, 2015 for an "evangelical agenda" piece explicating that position. As discussed in earlier chapters, there have been concerted attacks on trans*+ and nonbinary participation in society generated from within the Trump administration, and it is unlikely that these efforts will be abandoned even if these forces lose political power as Trump's personal political fortunes decline. Systematic and institutional oppression damages health and well-being whenever it occurs (Winter et al., 2016), and trans*+ and nonbinary people will continue to need allies to help them overcome these powerful forces. Allies can appear anywhere and can have immense impact. Trans*+ and nonbinary people have often been surprised when allies stand up with them, but that shouldn't be the case forever. The educational efforts that have been ongoing in this country since the 1960s are gaining ground and building more grassroots support for trans*+ and nonbinary people (Green, 2004).

Young people are often disheartened by national politics: everything seems so far away, the old power-brokers are so entrenched within the traditional establishment systems, there seems to be no hope of exerting influence. But there is hope. The efforts of young people to express themselves, to expand our understanding of gender and sex stereotyping in the law, to explore the pre-existing limits of either scientific or religious understandings of gender in the humanities through research or through art, and the movement-building that is on-going across the country, building on cooperative allyship among a host of well-positioned organizations, offers the next generation of leaders fertile ground for shaping gender's future. It's all waiting for you. Advocate for yourself; make a positive difference for others; change the world.

# Afterword

## Meredith Talusan

Since I began writing on trans-related issues five years ago, I've seen an enormous shift in people's understandings of the concepts and stakes involved, as well as the number of people who have been willing to take on the mantle of advocating for trans lives. Yet even with this greater awareness, and as I continue to be invited into rarefied contexts—whether universities, conferences, or board rooms—I am more often than not the only trans person there. And when there happen to be other trans people in these rooms, they tend to be predominantly white, as the burdens of bias and discrimination multiply the more minority identities one holds.

It's important to note, for instance, that there is a lack of racial-minority contributors to this volume, one that is also authored primarily by female-assigned people, in an academic context that can be exceedingly challenging for transfeminine folks to navigate. As Rhea Ashley Hoskin and her co-authors note in Chapter 4: "In a patriarchal society, perhaps it makes sense that someone assigned female would want to be a man, but to want to be a woman is considered pathological," and academic institutions are not immune to this unconscious logic. Overt femininity is coded in our culture as frivolous and unintellectual, yet for trans femmes, any sign of departure from a feminine ideal risks the worst effects of transphobia. I name these dynamics in this afterword to what I hope will be an extremely useful book not as a critique of *Navigating Trans*\*+ and Complex Gender Identities* itself, but the structures that produce it and the society that it can't help but be a part of, even as it aims to challenge and improve those structures.

Another reason why I name these dynamics is to break down the notion of allyship, both as it functions in this volume as well as out in the world. sj Miller writes in our preface, "This book ... is written to support the mainstream to become part of this re/evolution, but it isn't only written for those in mind. In fact, people with complex gender identities also want to know how to do the work and are seeking strategies to offer their networks." Distinguishing the mainstream from those with complex gender identities is important for defining two distinct communities this book addresses, but it is also vital to state that these groups break down as soon as we account for the necessarily intersectional nature of identity, not to mention that individual lives cannot be reduced to the summation of their identities.

Let me put it this way: the fact that you are here, reading this book, whether you're cis or trans, already defines you as mainstream compared to those who do not have access to this book. You are literate, are likely in a college setting, have been exposed to academic discourse, and have led a life free of the many obstacles that would have prevented you from being excluded from the knowledge contained here. Moreover, despite the fact that the contributors to this book are predominantly trans and all certainly have complex gender identities, we are in a privileged position compared to much of the trans and GNC community by virtue of simply being in a position to disseminate our ideas in the form of a book distributed by a large press.

Thus, the writers and readers of this book, regardless of gender, constitute a shared community that enjoys privileges those who don't have access to this book do not possess. In this sense, when Jamison Green declares, "We need allies! Allies bring a variety of strengths and capacities to any group's ability to reach goals," I believe that allyship is not only for cis people, but also for trans and gender-complex people who have greater access, such that they belong to the group of people who have access to this book. We all have the responsibility of allyship to members of the trans community who are deprived of material, educational, and social resources because of their identity.

Except that even as I wish to break down allyship as being only for cisgender people in relation to trans people, I believe that the notion of allyship itself comes with its own problems, because it relies on the idea that the oppressed are supposed to be the one who should rightfully advocate for ourselves, which itself is predicated on the pernicious ideology that we are ultimately responsible for the issues we face when we try to navigate our cisgender-dominated society. But the fact is that in the case of trans people, for instance, the root of our issues is not with being trans itself, but society's continued oppression of us, and that the perpetrators of that oppression are cisgender people.

As such, I don't consider allyship to be the most productive model to address this oppression. Allyship implies participation in a movement that one is not inherently a part of, but that one takes on as a matter of generosity. To me, this lets cisgender allies off the hook, as well as allies of other minority movements. Minorities are in fact the people who are most impacted by oppressive structures and non-minorities the most responsible, so any notion of allyship must be rooted not in a sense of altruism, but rather a much more urgent sense of moral obligation, so much so that the term "ally" itself cannot encompass its weight. Even when a cisgender ally has never participated actively in the oppression of trans and gender-nonconforming people, their mere existence is oppressive because the benefits they derive from being cisgender is dependent on trans people being deprived of the numerous social and material benefits cisgender people enjoy.

Even as a transfeminine, disabled, first-generation immigrant person of color, my own position as the writer of this afterword, regardless of whatever other personal qualities I have, cannot be divorced from the forces of tokenism that often attend those of us from severely disadvantaged backgrounds who gain access to exceptional opportunities. I feel a moral obligation to say that many of the opportunities I've been given and positions I've held have come to me because people and organizations see the necessity of a voice belonging to my demographic group, which has also meant that those positions are only meant for a single person of my kind, so I unavoidably deprive other trans femmes of color of opportunities simply by accepting them. I therefore consistently balance my desire to avail of opportunities for myself with the work of creating opportunities for other trans people. However, these losses of opportunity through tokenism are miniscule compared to the daily experience of multitudes of trans people who are rarely if ever preferred over cis people, whether in school or at work, as friends or as colleagues. You may never know whether you've deprived a trans person through your sheer existence, but there's a high probability you have, and a guarantee that people in more marginalized positions than you have suffered because of your place in the world.

It is in this sense that being an ally is not enough. After reading this book, I hope that you feel a strong moral obligation, as I do, not merely to imbibe its knowledge, but to practice it out in the world, to ensure that you have a tangible effect in bettering marginalized trans lives to the full extent of your capacity. And this practice must not merely come from a sense of goodness of virtue, but as a form of redress and reparation for the many ways that your very ability to have the resources to help other people is predicated on a social structure that unjustly rewards you while oppressing those people in the first place. By supporting trans and gender-complex people as we navigate the world, you won't merely do something good, you will do something right, and help repair injustices that should never have existed to begin with.

# Appendix A

## Cisgender Privilege Checklist

**Directions:** As you read the list below, identify the privileges about being cisgender that surprised you. These examples of cis-privilege are meant to be viewed as a self-assessment and are therefore written in the first person.

### Clothing

- Clothing works for me, more or less.
- I am a size and shape for which clothes I feel comfortable wearing are commonly made.
- There are clothes designed with bodies like mine in mind.
- If I am unable to find clothing that fits me well, I will still feel safe, and recognizable as my gender.

### Healthcare

- I expect access to healthcare.
- I cannot be denied health insurance on the basis of my gender.
- I expect medical forms to reflect choices regarding my gender.
- I expect that I will not be denied medical treatment by a doctor on the basis of my gender.
- My identity is not considered a mental pathology ("gender dysphoria" in the DSM V) by the psychological and medical establishments.
- Treatments that are medically necessary for me are generally covered by insurance.
- I expect that medical professionals competent to treat my conditions exist outside of major cities, and in proportion to the demand for them. I expect no undue delay in access to routine medical services, and for such services to be available (at least) five days a week.
- If I end up in the emergency room, I do not have to worry that my gender will keep me from receiving appropriate treatment, or that all of my medical issues will be seen as a result of my gender.
- I expect that there exists formal training about medical conditions affecting me.

- I am not required to undergo an extensive psychological evaluation in order to receive basic medical care.
- There is information about the prevalence of HIV/AIDS and other diseases in my community.

### Local and National Travel

- I expect my gender to not unduly affect my ability to travel nationally and internationally.
- If I am asked for a pat down by a TSA agent, I expect it to be done by a person who reflects my gender or I will be asked which agent I prefer.
- My gender presentation is legal in all countries.
- I expect that information on a country relevant to travelers of my gender will be readily available, and supplied to me by travel guides, travel agents, and study abroad officials.
- I expect that a visa and passport will be sufficient documentation for me to enter any country, however difficult these may be to obtain.
- I expect that my documentation will decrease suspicion about me.

### Media and the Arts

- Bodies like mine are represented in the media and the arts.
- Bodies like mine are represented in magazines and books.
- I can identify with images of my body in movies, plays, shows, etc.
- I see people like me on the news.
- I can easily find role models and mentors to emulate and who share my identity.
- Hollywood accurately depicts people of my gender in films and television, and does not solely make my identity the focus of a dramatic storyline, or the punchline for a joke.

### Offenses

- Wronging me is typically taken seriously.
  a. Those who wrong me are expected to know that it is hurtful, and are considered blameworthy whether or not they intended to wrong me.
  b. I have easy access to people who understand that this wrong is not acceptable, and who will support me.
  c. I have easy access to resources and people to educate someone who wronged me, if I am not feeling up to it.
  d. If I am being wronged, I can expect that others who are around will notice.

## Physical and Emotional Safety

- I do not expect to be physically assaulted because of my body.
- I do not expect someone to question that I am cisgender and if they do, that I would incur violence as a result.
- I do not expect to be demeaned or belittled because I am cisgender.
- I can reasonably assume that I will not be denied services at a hospital, bank, or other institution because the staff does not believe the gender marker on my ID card matches my gender identity.
- When someone checks my identification or my driver's license, I will never be insulted or glared at because my name or sex does not match the sex they believed me to be based on my gender expression.
- I do not expect strangers will ask me what my genitals look like or how I have sex.
- I can walk through the world with little concern for my safety and well-being and do not scan others in fear that I may be assaulted or mocked because of my body and/or appearance.
- If someone else thinks I'm in the wrong bathroom, locker room, or changing room, I am in no danger of verbal abuse, arrest, stares, or physical intimidation.
- When (or if) people mistake my gender, there are unlikely to be serious consequences.
- I have the ability to flirt, engage in courtship, or form a relationship and not fear that my biological status may be cause for rejection or attack, nor will it cause my partner to question their sexual orientation.
- When I am dating someone, I do not question if they aren't just looking to satisfy a curiosity or kink pertaining to my gender identity (e.g., the "novelty" of having sex with a trans person).
- I not have to defend my right to be a part of the "Queer" community, and gays and lesbians will not try to exclude me from "their" equal rights movement because of my gender identity (or any equality movement, including feminist rights).
- When I interact with law enforcement, I do not fear interactions with police officers due to my gender identity, nor do I fear that I may be provided differential treatment.
- If I am murdered (or have any crime committed against me), my gender expression will not be used as a justification for my murder ("gay or trans panic"), nor as a reason to coddle the perpetrators.

- I do not have to pretend that anatomy and gender are irrevocably entwined when having the "boy parts and girl parts" talk with children, instead of explaining the actual complexity of gender and sex.
- I don't have to convince my parents of my true gender and/or have to earn my parents' and siblings' love and respect all over again.
- I don't have to remind my extended family *over* and *over* to use proper gender pronouns or different names (e.g., after transitioning).

## Privacy
- I expect the privacy of my body to be respected in bathrooms, locker rooms, and changing facilities.
- My gender is always an option on a form.
- I am not asked about what my genitalia looks like, or whether or not my breasts are real, what medical procedures I have had, etc.
- It is easily possible for representations of my naked body to pass obscenity restrictions.
- I am not asked by others what my "real name is or was."
- I can reasonably assume that my ability to acquire a job, rent an apartment, or secure a loan will not be denied on the basis of my gender identity/ expression.
- I am able to go to places with friends on a whim knowing there will be bathrooms there I can use.

## Sex segregated facilities
*I expect access to, and fair treatment within:*
- Homeless shelters
- Domestic violence shelters
- Dormitories
- Drug rehabilitation
- Prisons
- Bathrooms
- Locker rooms
- Gyms
- Hostels
- Juvenile justice systems

**Workplace**

- I expect laws banning the creation of a hostile work environment will ban the use of offensive language about me.
- I expect laws to be in place that prevent sexual or gender-type harassment.
- I expect to have a bathroom that I can use without fear of physical or verbal intimidation, stares, or ridicule.

# Appendix B

**Exercises for practicing names and pronouns:**

The "Get to Know Me" allows students to privately reveal their *current* claimed name, (a)gender identity (i.e., gender identity or absence thereof), and, (a)pronouns (i.e., pronouns or absence thereof), and has an option to note if they want these identities publicly acknowledged. For the student who does not want others to know about particular identities, but is comfortable sharing that part of the self with the educator, the educator can respond on assignments with comments that recognize the student's true name, (a)gender identity, and or (a)pronoun.

My assigned name is _____ and my claimed name (leave blank if they are the same) is _____. My assigned sex is _____ but my CURRENT, claimed (a)gender identity (leave blank if they are the same) is _____. The pronouns people use when referring to me include _____ but my CURRENT, claimed (a)pronoun is/are _____.

In class I prefer you to use (please circle) *assigned* or *claimed* <u>name</u>, *assigned* or *claimed* <u>(a)pronouns</u>, but on my assignments, you can use (please circle) *assigned or claimed* <u>name</u> and *assigned or claimed* <u>(a)pronouns</u>.

# Appendix C

Do **you** use *pronouns*?

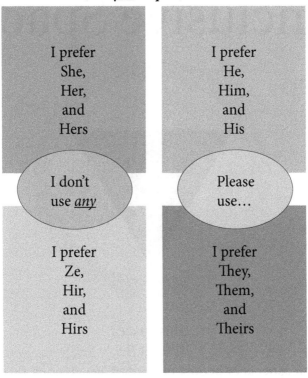

I prefer
She,
Her,
and
Hers

I prefer
He,
Him,
and
His

I don't
use *any*

Please
use…

I prefer
Ze,
Hir,
and
Hirs

I prefer
They,
Them,
and
Theirs

**Appendix C** Pronoun chart

# Appendix D

# Inclusive Space

This space
RESPECTS
all aspects of people including age, gender, race,
ethnicity, religion/no religion, national origin,
immigration status, language, education, marital status,
body size, political affiliation/philosophy, (a)sexual
orientation, (a)gender identity/expression and
creativity, physical and mental ability, social-economic
status, genetic information, medical status, veteran
status, and the indeterminate.

**Appendix D** Inclusive space sign

# Appendix E

## Gender, Pronouns, and Romantic Orientations List

**Gender Master List: (gender may be made into *boy, girl, nonbinary*, etc.)**
**(example: demigender, demiboy, demigirl, demi-nonbinary)**

*Abimegender:* a gender that is profound, deep, and infinite; meant to resemble when one mirror is reflecting into another mirror creating an infinite paradox

**Adamasgender:** a gender which refuses to be categorized

**Aerogender:** a gender that is influenced by your surroundings

**Aesthetigender:** a gender that is derived from an aesthetic; also known as *videgender*

**Affectugender:** a gender that is affected by mood swings

**Agender:** the feeling of having no gender/absence of gender or neutral gender

**Agenderflux:** being mostly *agender* except having small shifts towards other genders making them *demigenders* (because of the constancy of being agender)

**Alexigender:** a gender that is fluid between more than one gender but the individual cannot tell what those genders are

**Aliusgender:** a gender that is removed from common gender descriptors and guidelines

**Amaregender:** a gender that changes depending on who you're in love with

**Ambigender:** defined as having the feeling of two genders simultaneously without fluctuation; meant to reflect the concept of being ambidextrous, only with gender

**Ambonec:** identifying as both man and woman, yet neither at the same time

**Amicagender:** a gender that changes depending on which friend you're with

**Androgyne:** sometimes used in the case of "androgynous presentation"; describes the feeling of being a mix of both masculine and feminine (and sometimes neutral) gender qualities

**Anesigender:** feeling like a certain gender yet being more comfortable identifying with another

**Angenital:** a desire to be without primary sexual characteristics, without necessarily being genderless; one may be both angenital and identify as any other gender alongside

**Anogender:** a gender that fades in and out but always comes back to the same feeling

**Anongender:** a gender that is unknown to both yourself and others

**Antegender:** a protean gender that has the potential to be anything, but is formless and motionless and, therefore, does not manifest as any particular gender

**Anxiegender:** a gender that is affected by anxiety

**Apagender:** a feeling of apathy towards one's gender that leads to their not looking any further into it

**Apconsugender:** a gender where you know what it isn't, but not what it is; the gender is hiding itself from you

**Astergender:** a gender that feels bright and celestial

**Astralgender:** a gender that feels connected to space

**(POSSIBLE TRIGGER WARNING) Autigender:** a gender that can only be understood in the context of being autistic

**Autogender:** a gender experience that is deeply personal to oneself

**Axigender:** when a person experiences two genders that sit on opposite ends of an axis; one being agender and the other being any other gender; these genders are experienced one at a time with no overlapping and with very short transition time

**Bigender:** the feeling of having two genders either at the same time or separately; usually used to describe feeling "traditionally male" and "traditionally female," but does not have to

**Biogender:** a gender that feels connected to nature in some way

**Blurgender:** the feeling of having more than one gender that are somehow blurred together to the point of not being able to distinguish or identify individual genders; synonymous with *genderfuzz*

**Boyflux:** when one feels mostly or all male most of the time but experience fluctuating intensity of male identity

**Burstgender:** gender that comes in intense bursts of feeling and quickly fades back to the original state

**Caelgender:** a gender that shares qualities with outer space or has the aesthetic of space, stars, nebulas, etc.

**Cassgender:** the feeling of gender is unimportant to you

**Cassflux:** when the level of indifference toward your gender fluctuates

**Cavusgender:** for people with depression; when you feel one gender when not depressed and another when depressed

**Cendgender:** when your gender changes between one and its opposite

**Ceterofluid:** when you are ceterogender and your feelings fluctuate between masculine, feminine, and neutral

**Ceterogender:** a nonbinary gender with specific masculine, feminine, or neutral feelings

**Cisgender:** the feeling of being the gender you were assigned at birth, all the time (assigned [fe]male/feeling [fe]male)

**Cloudgender:** a gender that cannot be fully realized or seen clearly due to depersonalization/derealization disorder

**Collgender:** the feeling of having too many genders simultaneously to describe each one

**Colorgender:** a gender associated with one or more colors and the feelings, hues, emotions, and/or objects associated with that color; may be used like pinkgender, bluegender, yellowgender

**Commogender:** when you know you aren't cisgender, but you have settled with your assigned gender for the time being

**Condigender:** a gender that is only felt during certain circumstances

**Deliciagender:** from the Latin word *delicia* meaning "favorite," meaning the feeling of having more than one simultaneous gender yet preferring one that fits better

**Demifluid:** the feeling your gender being fluid throughout all the demigenders; the feeling of having multiple genders, some static and some fluid

**Demiflux:** the feeling of having multiple genders, some static and some fluctuating

**Demigender:** a gender that is partially one gender and partially another

**Domgender:** having more than one gender yet one being more dominant than the others

**Demi-vapor (term coined by @cotton-blossom-jellyfish):** Continuously drifting to other genders, feeling spiritually transcendental when doing so while having a clear—slightly blurred—inner visual of your genders, transitions, and positive emotions. Tied to Demi-smoke.

**Demi-smoke (term coined by @cotton-blossom-jellyfish):** A transcendental, spiritual gender roughly drifting to other genders that are unable to be foreseen and understood, shrouded in darkness within your inner visual. Elevating through mystery. Caused by a lack of inner interpretation and dark emotional states. Tied to Demi-vapor.

**Duragender:** from the Latin word *dura* meaning "long-lasting," meaning a subcategory of *multigender* in which one gender is more identifiable, long lasting, and prominent than the other genders

**Egogender:** a gender that is so personal to your experience that it can only be described as "you"

**Epicene:** sometimes used synonymously with the adjective "androgynous"; the feeling of either having or not displaying characteristics of both or either binary gender; sometimes used to describe feminine male-identifying individuals

**Espigender:** a gender that is related to being a spirit or exists on a higher or extradimensional plane

**Exgender:** the outright refusal to accept or identify in, on, or around the gender spectrum

**Existigender:** a gender that only exists or feels present when thought about or when a conscious effort is made to notice it

**Femfluid:** having fluctuating or fluid gender feelings that are limited to feminine genders

**Femgender:** a nonbinary gender that is feminine in nature

**Fluidflux:** the feeling of being fluid between two or more genders that also fluctuate in intensity; a combination of *genderfluid* and *genderflux*

**Gemigender:** having two opposite genders that work together, being fluid and flux together

**Genderblank:** a gender that can only be described as a blank space; when gender is called into question, all that comes to mind is a blank space

**Genderflow:** a gender that is fluid between infinite feelings

**Genderfluid:** the feeling of fluidity within your gender identity; feeling a different gender as time passes or as situations change; not restricted to any number of genders

**Genderflux:** the feeling of your gender fluctuating in intensity; like *genderfluid* but between one gender and *agender*

**Genderfuzz: (term coined by lolzmelmel):** the feeling of having more than one gender that are somehow blurred together to the point of not being able to distinguish or identify individual genders; synonymous with *blurgender*

**Gender Neutral:** the feeling of having a neutral gender, whether somewhere in between masculine and feminine or a third gender that is separate from the binary; often paired with *neutrois*

**Genderpunk:** a gender identity that actively resists gender norms

**Genderqueer:** originally used as an umbrella term for nonbinary individuals; may be used as an identity; describes a nonbinary gender regardless of whether the individual is masculine or feminine leaning

**Genderwitched:** a gender in which one is intrigued or entranced by the idea of a particular gender, but is not certain that they are actually feeling it

**Girlflux:** when one feels mostly or all female most of the time but experiences fluctuating intensities of female identity

**Glassgender:** a gender that is very sensitive and fragile

**Glimragender:** a faintly shining, wavering gender

**Greygender:** having a gender that is mostly outside of the binary but is weak and can barely be felt

**Gyragender:** having multiple genders but understanding none of them

**Healgender:** a gender that, once realized, brings lots of peace, clarity, security, and creativity to the individual's mind

**Heliogender:** a gender that is warm and burning

**Hemigender:** a gender that is half one gender and half something else; one or both halves may be identifiable genders

**Horogender:** a gender that changes over time with the core feeling remaining the same

**Hydrogender:** a gender which shares qualities with water

**Imperigender:** a fluid gender that can be controlled by the individual

**Intergender:** the feeling of gender falling somewhere on the spectrum between masculine and feminine; note: do not confuse with *intersex*

**Juxera:** a feminine gender similar to girl, but on a separate plane and off to itself

**Libragender:** a gender that feels *agender* but has a strong connection to another gender

**Magigender:** a gender that is mostly gender and the rest is something else

**Mascfluid:** A gender that is fluid in nature, and restricted only to masculine genders

**Mascgender:** a nonbinary gender that is masculine in nature.

**Maverique:** taken from the word "maverick"; the feeling of having a gender that is separate from masculinity, femininity, and neutrality, but is not agender; a form of third gender

**Mirrorgender:** a gender that changes to fit the people around you

**Molligender:** a gender that is soft, subtle, and subdued

**Multigender:** the feeling of having more than one simultaneous or fluctuating gender; simultaneous with *multigender* and *omnigender*

**Nanogender:** feeling a small part of one gender with the rest being something else

**Neutrois:** the feeling of having a neutral gender; sometimes a lack of gender that leads to feeling neutral

**Nonbinary:** originally an umbrella term for any gender outside the binary of cisgenders; may be used as an individual identity; occasionally used alongside of *genderqueer*

**Omnigender:** the feeling of having more than one simultaneous or fluctuating gender; simultaneous with *multigender* and *polygender*

**Oneirogender:** being agender, but having recurring fantasies or daydreams of being a certain gender without the dysphoria or desire to actually be that gender day-to-day

**Pangender:** the feeling of having every gender; this is considered problematic by some communities and thus has been used as the concept of relating in some way to all genders as opposed to containing every gender identity; only applies to genders within one's own culture

**Paragender:** the feeling of being very near one gender, and partially something else that keeps you from feeling fully that gender

**Perigender:** identifying with a gender but not as a gender

**Polygender:** the feeling of having more than one simultaneous or fluctuating gender; simultaneous with *multigender* and *omnigender*

**Proxvir:** a masculine gender similar to boy, but on a separate plane and off to itself

**Quoigender:** feeling as if the concept of gender is inapplicable or nonsensical to one's self

**Subgender:** mostly *agender* with a bit of another gender

**Surgender:** having a gender that is 100% one gender but with more of another gender added on top of that

**Systemgender:** a gender that is the sum of all the genders within a multiple or median system

**Tragender:** a gender that stretches over the whole spectrum of genders

**Transgender:** any gender identity that transcends or does not align with your assigned gender or society's idea of gender; the feeling of being any gender that does not match your assigned gender

**Trigender:** the feeling of having three simultaneous or fluctuating genders

**Vapogender:** a gender that sort of feels like smoke; can be seen on a shallow level but once you go deeper, it disappears and you are left with no gender and only tiny wisps of what you thought it was

**Venngender:** when two genders overlap creating an entirely new gender; like a venn diagram

**Verangender:** a gender that seems to shift/change the moment it is identified

**Vibragender:** a gender that is usually one stable gender but will occasionally change or fluctuate before stabilizing again

**Vocigender:** a gender that is weak or hollow

## Pronoun Master List

1.  *e/h*/h*s/h*self
2.  ae/aer/aers/aerself
3.  ce/cir/cirs/cirself
4.  co/cos/cos/coself
5.  e/em/eir/emself
6.  ey/eim/eir/eirself
7.  ey/em/eir/emself
8.  fey/fer/fers/ferself
9.  fey/feys/feyself
10. fey/feyr/feyself
11. fir/firs/firself
12. he/him/his/himself
13. hir/hir/hirs/hirself
14. hu/hu/hume/humeself
15. it/it/its/itself (only if explicitly told this is okay)
16. jee/jem/jeir/jemself
17. jam/jam/jams/jamself
18. jhey/jhem/jheir/jheirself
19. kye/kyr/kyne/kyrself
20. kir/kir/kirs/kirself
21. lee/lim/lis/limself
22. mae/mair/maes/maeself
23. ne/nem/neir/neirself
24. ne/nem/nir/nemself
25. ne/nis/nimself
26. ne/nym/nis/nymself
27. per/per/pers/perself
28. she/her/hers/herself
29. she/sheer/sheers/sheerself
30. sie/sier/siers/sierself

31. sie/hir/hirself
32. ou/ou/ous/ouself
33. tey/tem/ter/temself
34. they/them/their/themself
35. thae/thaer/thaers/thaerself
36. this one/ that one
37. thon/thon/thons/thonself
38. ve/vir/virs/virself
39. ve/vis/vir/verself
40. xe/hir/hirs/hirself
41. xe/xim/xis/ximself
42. xe/xir/xirs/xirself
43. xie/xem/xyr/xemself
44. xe/xem/xyr/xyrself
45. yre/yres/yreself
46. zay/zir/zirs/zirself
47. ze(or zie)/zir/zirs/zirself
48. ze/hir/hirs/hirself
49. ze/zir/zirs/zirself
50. ze/zan/zan/zanself
51. zed/zed/zeds/zedself
52. zed/zed/zeir/zedself
53. zhe/zhim/zhir/zhirself
54. zhe/zhir/zhirs/zhirself

## Orientation Master List

There are six types of attraction.

- **sexual**: "I want to have sex with you"
- **romantic**: "I want to date you"
- **sensual**: "I want to hug/kiss you"
- **platonic**: "I want to be friends with you"
- **aesthetic**: "You look nice"
- **alterous**: "I feel an emotional connection that is indeterminate" (can best be described as desiring emotional closeness with someone; is neither platonic nor romantic but rather somewhere inbetween the two)

*All types of attractions may be used as suffixes along with "-fluid" and*
*"-flux". Mix and match prefixes and suffixes to create an orientation.*

**A-** : lack of attraction

**Abro-** : having an orientation or feelings about it that constantly change and
cannot be pinned down for this reason

**Aceflux:** similar to genderflux where the intensity of sexual attraction you feel
fluctuates; *asexual* to *demisexual* to *allosexual* and back

**Aego-** : feeling attraction or desire only for situations that do not involve
oneself; previously known as *autochoris-*

**Akoi-** : the feeling of attraction but not wanting it reciprocated or losing
it when it is reciprocated; used as an alternative and potentially less
problematic form of *lithosexual/lithoromantic*

**Aliqua-** : not normally feeling attraction, but feeling it on occasion under
specific circumstances

**Amicus-** : when you're attracted to people you're platonically attracted to

**Amorplatonic:** experiencing romantic attraction but only wanting to be in
queerplatonic/quasiplatonic relationships

**Apothi-** : being *aromantic/asexual* and not experiencing any romantic/sexual
feelings in any shape or form; aromantic/asexual individuals who are
romance/sex repulsed

**Aromantic:** feeling no romantic attraction regardless of gender or situation

**Aroflux:** similar to genderflux where the intensity or romantic attraction you
feel fluctuates; *aromantic* to *demiromantic* to *alloromantic* and back

**Arospike/Acespike:** feeling no attraction except in occasional bursts of
intense attraction and then plummeting back to no attraction

**Asexual:** feeling no sexual attraction regardless of gender or situation

**Auto-** : the feeling of attraction only toward oneself

**Bellusromantic:** having interest in conventionally romantic things yet not
desiring a relationship; part of the aro spectrum

**Bi-** : the feeling of attraction toward two or more genders, generally your own
gender and other(s)

**Borea-** : having an exception to your usual orientation

**Burst-** : having spikes in attraction that fade away after a while

**Cass-** : feeling utterly indifferent toward attraction and believing it's not important

**Cease-** : usually being allo- yet occasionally feeling a sudden loss of attraction
and then returning to normal

**Cetero-** : the feeling of attraction toward nonbinary people; replaces *skolio-*
because "skolio" means bent or broken and implies that nonbinary people

must be fixed; this is reserved for trans/nonbinary individuals because cis people were judging nonbinary people based on presentation alone

**Culparomantic:** feeling romantic and platonic attraction at the same time

**Cupio- :** the feeling of having no attraction toward any gender yet still desiring a sexual or romantic relationship

**Demi- :** not feeling attraction toward someone until a certain closeness or bond has been formed

**Desinoromantic:** when one does not experience full-on romantic attraction, but experiences "liking" someone instead of loving them romantically, at which point the attraction goes no further

**Duo- :** having two or more well-defined orientations that you switch between

**Ficto- :** only feeling a certain type of attraction toward fictional characters

**Fin- :** feeling attraction to fem(me) identifying people

**Fray- :** only experiencing attraction toward those you are less familiar with; the feeling is lost when they become closer or more familiar; the opposite of *demi-*

**Grey- :** the feeling of usually not having any attraction except occasionally depending on the situation; typically paired with *asexual* and *aromantic*

**Heteroflexible:** the feeling of having mostly hetero- attraction yet having an openness for other genders

**Hetero- :** the feeling of being attracted to a gender other than your own

**Homoflexible:** the feeling of having mostly homo- attraction yet having an openness for other genders

**Homo- :** the feeling of being attracted to your own gender

**Iculasexual:** being asexual but open to having sex

**Idemromantic:** being able to categorize others as having either a platonic or romantic attraction based on outside factors yet feeling no difference in the type of attraction

**Kalossexual:** the desire to have a sexual relationship yet never feeling sexual attraction; part of the ace spectrum

**Lamvano- :** feeling no desire to do sexual/romantic things to someone, but wanting to be on the receiving end; opposite of placio-

**Lesbian:** someone who identifies fully or partially as a woman who is attracted to other fully or partially identified women

**Limno- :** experiencing attraction toward depictions of attraction (writing or drawings) but not the physical acts

**Ma- :** feeling attraction to men

**Min-** : feeling attraction to masculine-identifying people

**Multi-** : attraction to more than one gender

**Neu-** : feeling attraction toward people who are genderless

**Nin-** : feeling attraction toward androgynous-identifying people

**Nocisma-** : feeling attraction to everyone except cismen because of associated oppression

**Noma-** : experiencing attraction to every gender except for self-identifying men

**Novi-** : feeling complicated attraction or lack thereof in such a way that it is difficult or impossible to fit into one word or term

**Novo-** : when one's orientation changes with gender

**Nowo-** : experiencing attraction to every gender except for self-identifying women

**Omni-** : the feeling of a lack of preference in gender; may be attracted to all genders equally; similar to *pan-*

**Pan-** : the feeling of attraction toward any gender or all genders; similar to *omni-*

**Penulti-** : feeling attraction toward every gender except your own

**Platoniromantic:** feeling no difference between platonic and romantic attraction

**Polar-** : feeling either extreme attraction or intense repulsion

**Poly-** : the feeling of attraction toward most or several genders (but not all)

**Pomo-** : the feeling of having no orientation

**Pre-** : a placeholder term for someone who doesn't think they've experienced enough attraction to know their orientation

**Proqua-** : feeling attracted to feminine people when you yourself are feminine

**Proquu-** : feeling attracted to masculine people when you yourself are masculine

**Queer:** the feeling of not being hetero- yet not wanting to further identify with any conventional sexuality

**Quoiromantic:** from the French word "quoi" meaning "what"; the feeling of not being able to distinguish romantic from platonic attraction and therefore being unsure if one has experienced it; used to replace wtfromantic because of vulgarity

**Recip-** : the feeling of only experiencing attraction once someone else has experienced it toward them first

**Requies-** : not feeling attraction when emotionally exhausted

**Sans-** : when there's no trend line in the attraction one feels, it just does what it does

**Sensu-** : an orientation that is based on sensuality as opposed to romance, sexuality, etc; different from sensual orientation; when romantic or sexual-type pleasure is derived from sensual acts or situations

**Skolio-** : the feeling of attraction toward nonbinary genders; replaced by *cetero-* because of problematic wording

**Specio-** : feeling attraction toward someone based on specific traits, not gender

**Thym-** : feeling attraction that varies depending on emotional state

**Volit-** : feeling attraction that is not directed at anyone in particular

**Woma-** : feeling attraction to women

# Appendix F

## Gender Identity and Cisgender Audit

### Audit of Gender Identity Awareness

| Observation | Describe gender markers | Self or Other (who is doing the thinking about the observation)? | Who is reinforcing? | Location |
|---|---|---|---|---|
| Girl on cereal | Pigtails, pink shirt, etc. | Other | Corporation | House |
| "Yes, miss" | Presumption that I'm female because of my mannerisms, hair, voice. | Self | Professor in class | University campus |

## Audit of Cisgender Awareness

| Observation | Describe cisgender normativity | Self or Other (who is doing the thinking about the observation)? | Who is reinforcing? | Location |
|---|---|---|---|---|
| "Referred to as ma'am or sir" | • I expect access to healthcare.<br>• I expect medical forms to reflect choices regarding my gender.<br>• I am not required to undergo an extensive psychological evaluation in order to receive basic medical care. | Self | Doctor, nurse, receptionist | Doctor's office |
| "Someone says hi" | • I can walk through the world with little concern for my safety and well-being and do not scan others in fear that I may be assaulted or mocked because of my body and/or appearance.<br>• I do not expect to be physically assaulted because of my body. | Self | Person on trail | On a hike |
| Notices someone who might be otherly gendered in the same bathroom | • I expect the privacy of my body to be respected in bathrooms, locker rooms, and changing facilities.<br>• I am able to go to places with friends on a whim knowing there will be bathrooms there I can use. | Other | Older woman in bathroom | Bathroom at mall |

# Appendix G

## Glossary of Terms: Defining a Common Queer Language

**(A)gender or agender** Rejecting gender as a biological or social construct altogether and refusing to identify with gender.

**(A)gender and (a)sexual justice and queer autonomy** These interchangeable terms each ideologically reflect an actualized freedom of humans to be self-expressive without fear of social, institutional, or political violence. See also *queer autonomy*.

**(A)gender self-determination** This is the inherent right to both occupy one's (a)gender and make choices to self-identify in a way that authenticates self-expression. It is also a type of self-granted or inherited permission that can help one refute or rise above social critique; it presumes choice and rejects an imposition to be defined or regulated; it presumes that humans are entitled to unsettle knowledge, which can generate new possibilities of legibility; and, it means that any representation of (a)gender deserves the same inalienable rights and the same dignities and protections as any other human. This "de factoness" grants individuals ways of intervening in and disrupting social and political processes because one's discourse and self-determined ways of being demonstrate placement as a viable stakeholder in society, revealing that no one personhood is of any more or less of value than any other.

**Ally** Any non-lesbian, non-gay man, non-bisexual, or cisgender person whose attitude and behavior are anti-heterosexist and who is proactive and works toward combating homophobia, transphobia, and heterosexism on both a personal and institutional level.

**Apronoun** Refusal of using pronouns when self-identifying.

**Aromantic** One who lacks a romantic orientation or is incapable of feeling romantic attraction. Aromantics can still have a sexual orientation (e.g., "aromantic bisexual" or "aromantic heterosexual"). A person who feels neither romantic nor sexual attraction is known as an aromantic asexual.

**Asexual/Ace** A person who does not experience sexual attraction to another person. Individuals may still be emotionally, physically, romantically, and/or spiritually attracted to others, and their romantic orientation may also be lesbian, gay, bisexual, transgender*⁺, intersex, agender/asexual, gender creative, queer, and questioning (LGBT*⁺IAGCQQ) (A in this case meaning ally). The prefixes of homo-, hetero-, bi-, pan-, poly-, demi-, and a- have been used to form terms such as heteroromantic, biromantic, homoromantic asexual, and so on. Unlike celibacy, which people choose, asexuality is intrinsic. Some asexual people do engage in sexual activity for a variety of reasons, such as a desire to please romantic partners or to have children.

**Assigned gender** The gender one is presumed or expected to embody based on assigned sex at birth.

**Assigned pronouns** The commonly accepted pronouns that others use to describe or refer to a person based on actual or perceived gender.

**Assigned sex** The sex one is assigned at birth based on genitalia.

**Bigender** Refers to those who have masculine and feminine sides to their personality. This is often a term used by cross dressers. It should not be confused with the term two-spirit, which is specifically a term used by Native Americans.

**Bisexuality/BI** A sexual orientation in which a person feels physically and emotionally attracted to both genders.

**Butch** An identity or presentation that leans toward masculinity. Butch can be an adjective ("she's a butch woman"), a verb ("he went home to butch up"), or a noun ("they identify as a butch"). Although commonly associated with masculine queer/lesbian women, it's used by many to describe a distinct gender identity and/or expression, and does not necessarily imply that one identifies as a woman.

**CAFAB and CAMAB** Acronyms meaning "Coercively Assigned Female/Male at Birth." Sometimes AFAB/FAAB and AMAB/MAAB (without the word "coercively") are used instead. No one, whether cis- or trans, has a choice in the sex or gender to which they are assigned when they are born, which is why it is said to be coercive. In the rare cases in which it is necessary to refer to the birth-assigned sex of a trans person, this is the way to do it.

**Cisgender or Cissexual** A person who by nature or by choice conforms to gender based expectations of society. (Also referred to as "genderstraight" or "Gender Normative.") A prefix of Latin origin, meaning "on the same side (as)." Cisgender individuals have a gender identity that is aligned with their birth sex, and therefore have a self-perception and gender expression that matches behaviors and roles considered appropriate for their birth sex: for example, a person who is feminine-identified that was born female. In short, cisgender is the opposite of transgender. It is important to recognize that even if two people identify as men (one being cis and the other being trans*), they may lead very similar lives but deal with different struggles pertaining to their birth sex.

**Cissexism** Synonymous with transphobia, this definition is associated with negative attitudes and feelings toward transgender people, based on the expression of their internal gender identity. Cissexism is also the belief that cisgender individuals are superior to transgender people and that a cisgender lifestyle is more desirable to lead.

**Claimed gender** The gender one feels most comfortable embodying and how one sees the self.

**Claimed pronouns or Claimed gender pronouns** This refers to names and pronouns that one feels most comfortable identifying with or being used when spoken or referred to. Names and pronouns can change over time and based on context and should be honored. Names and pronouns are ever-expanding and indeterminate. Examples might include: "ze", "per", they, "or "hir."

**Coming out** Also, "coming out of the closet" or "being out," this term refers to the process in which a person acknowledges, accepts, and in many cases appreciates her or his lesbian, gay, bisexual, or transgender identity. This often involves sharing of this information with others. It is not a single event but instead a life-long process. Each new situation poses the decision of whether or not to come out.

**Crip** Increasingly used to refer to a person who has a disability and embraces it, rather than feeling sorry for themselves. Historically used as a disparaging term for a person that is partially disabled or unable to use a limb or limbs. It is similar to the word queer in that it is sometimes used as a hateful slur, so although some have reclaimed it from their oppressors, be careful with its use.

**Cross-dressing (CD)** The act of dressing and presenting as the "opposite" binary gender. One who considers this an integral part of their identity may identify as a cross-dresser. "Transvestite" is an obsolete (and sometimes offensive) term with the same meaning. Cross-dressing and drag are forms of gender expression and are not necessarily tied to erotic activity, nor are they indicative of one's sexual orientation. Do NOT use these terms to describe someone who has transitioned or intends to do so in the future.

**Demisexual** A demisexual is a person who does not experience sexual attraction unless they form a strong emotional connection with someone. It's more commonly seen in but by no means confined to romantic relationships. The term demisexual comes from the orientation being "halfway between" sexual and asexual. Nevertheless, this term does not mean that demisexuals have an incomplete or half-sexuality, nor does it mean that sexual attraction without emotional connection is required for a complete sexuality. In general, demisexuals are not sexually attracted to anyone of any gender; however, when a demisexual is emotionally connected to someone else (whether the feelings are romantic love or deep friendship), the demisexual experiences sexual attraction and desire, but only toward the specific partner or partners.

**Drag** Stylized performance of gender, usually female-bodied drag kings or male-bodied drag queens. Doing drag does not necessarily have anything to do with one's sex, gender identity, or orientation.

**Femme** An identity or presentation that leans towards femininity. Femme can be an adjective ("he's a femmeboy"), a verb ("she feels better when she femmes up"), or a noun ("they're a femme"). Although commonly associated with feminine lesbian/queer women, it's used by many to describe a distinct gender identity and/or expression, and does not necessarily imply that one identities as a woman.

**Gay** A common and acceptable word for male homosexuals, but used for both genders.

**Gender** Socially constructed roles, behaviors, and attributes considered by the general public to be "appropriate" for one's sex as assigned at birth. Gender roles vary among cultures and along time continuums.

**Gender affirmation/confirmation surgery** Having surgery as means to construct genitalia of choice. Surgery does not change one's sex or gender, only genitalia. Gender/genitalia reassignment/reconstruction surgeries affirm an essentialist perspective of being born in the wrong sex from birth and are less frequently used in a lexicon.

**Gender attribution** Is the process by which an observer decides which gender they believe another person to be.

**Gender binary** A system of viewing gender as consisting solely of two categories (termed "woman" and "man") that are biologically based (female and male) and unchangeable, and in which no other possibilities for gender or anatomy are believed to exist. This system is oppressive to anyone who defines their birth assignment, but particularly those who are gender-variant people and do not fit neatly into one of the two categories.

**Gender creative** Expressing gender in a way that demonstrates individual freedom of expression and that does not conform to any gender.

**Gender dynamic/evolving/expansive** The recognition that gender continues to shift and emerge and generate pathways to understanding expansive views of gender. These new iterations of gender will continue to push on norms and stereotypes in ways that mean individuals can self-determine and have agency over their identities.

**Gender expression/presentation** The physical manifestation of one's gender identity through clothing, hairstyle, voice, body shape, etc., typically referred to as feminine or masculine. Many transgender people seek to make their gender expression (how they look) match their gender identity rather than their birth-assigned sex.

**Gender-fluid** Individuals who are between identifying with a gender or who do not identify with a gender. This term overlaps with genderqueer and bigender, implying movement between gender identities and/or presentations.

**Gender identity** This is the soul and spirit of a person: it is how an individual feels about themselves (Levine, 2008), intuits, and then writes themselves into the world (Perl, 2004). Gender identity is how someone wants to be seen and legitimated through the eyes of another in the world—just as someone *is* (Federal Intragency Working Group, 2016; Herbert, 2016).[3] Understood and fashioned in these ways, gender identity can be the embodiment of gender, or lack thereof, and any expressions of the self are reinforced by how we think and want others to see and think of ourselves. Gender identity can therefore be the physical, emotional, and/or psychological embodiment that rejects gender (*agender*) altogether.

**Gender identity complexity** The constant integration of new ideas and concepts and the invention of new knowledges—comprised of multitudes, and/or a moving away or sometimes a refusal to accept historically conferred constructions of binaries, genders, and bodies. Yet, in simultaneity, gender identity can be some of these, all of these, and none of these. It evades and resists categorization. *Synonyms*: Complex gender identity/identities, gender identity complex, or the complexity/complexities of gender identity/identities.

**Gender identity justice** The state of recognition in which all gender identities are afforded the same dignities as any other individual.

**Gender identity self-determination** The state of, and right to, self-identify in a way that authenticates one's self-expression and self-acceptance, and which refuses to be externally controlled, defined, or regulated.

**Gender non-conforming** A term for individuals whose gender expression is different from societal expectations related to gender.

**Gender Normativity** This is an expression of identity that aligns with social expectations and norms for one's gender. Cisgender, cissexual, and genderstraight are considered synonyms.

**Gender role/expression** How one performs gender in the world as it relates to social expectations and norms.

**Genderqueer** Those rejecting binary roles and language for gender. A general term for nonbinary gender identities. Those who identify as genderqueer may identify as neither woman nor man; may see themselves as outside of the binary gender boxes; may fall somewhere between the binary genders; or may reject the use of gender labels. Genderqueer identities fall under the "trans umbrella." Synonyms include androgynous.

**Gray-A Sexual** Asexuality and sexuality are not black and white; some people identify in the **gray** (spelled "**grey**" in some countries) area between them. People who identify as **gray-A** can include, but are not limited to those who: do not normally experience sexual attraction, but do experience it sometimes, experience sexual attraction, but a low sex drive, experience sexual attraction and drive, but not strongly enough to want to act on them, **and** people who can enjoy and desire sex, but only under very limited and specific circumstances. A person can be gray-heterosexual, gray-homosexual, and/or gray-bisexual.

**GSM** Gender and Sexual Minority is a term used to describe those who fall outside of dominant gender and sexuality identities.

**Hate Crime** Any act of intimidation, harassment, physical force or threat of physical force directed against any person, or their property, motivated either in whole or in part by hostility toward their actual or perceived age, disability, gender identity, ethnic background, race, religious/spiritual belief, sex, sexual orientation, etc.

**Heteroflexible** Similar to bisexual, but with a stated heterosexual preference. Sometimes characterized as being "mostly straight." Commonly used to indicate that one is interested in heterosexual romance but is "flexible" when it comes to sex and/or play. The same concepts apply to homoflexible.

**Heteronormative/Heteronormativity** A culture or belief system that assumes that people fall into distinct and complementary sexes and genders and that heterosexuality is the normal sexual orientation. A heteronormative view is one that involves alignment of biological sex, sexuality, gender identity, and gender roles, sexuality, gender identity, and gender roles.

**Heterosexism** The assumption that all people are or should be heterosexual. Heterosexism excludes the needs, concerns, and life experiences of lesbian, gay and bisexual people while it gives advantages to heterosexual people. It is often a subtle form of oppression that reinforces realities of silence and invisibility.

**Heterosexuality** A sexual orientation in which a person feels physically and emotionally attracted to people of the opposite gender.

**Homonormative/Homonormativity** The assimilation of heteronormative ideals and constructs into LGBT*+IAGCQQ culture and identity. Homonormativity upholds neoliberalism rather than critiquing monogamy, procreation, normative family social roles, and binary gender roles. It is criticized as undermining citizens' rights and erasing the historic alliance between radical politics and gay politics, the core concern being sexual freedom. Some assert that homonormativity fragments LGBT*+IAGCQQ communities into hierarchies of worthiness: those that mimic heteronormative standards of gender identity are deemed most worthy of receiving rights. Individuals at the bottom of the hierarchy are seen as an impediment to this elite class of homonormative individuals receiving their rights. Because LGBT*+IAGCQQ activists and organizations embrace systems that endorse normative family social roles and serial monogamy, some believe that LGBT*+IAGCQQ people are surrendering and conforming to heteronormative behavior.

**Homophobia** The fear, dislike, and/or hatred of same-sex relationships or those who love and are sexually attracted to those of the same sex. Homophobia includes prejudice, discrimination, harassment, and acts of violence brought on by fear and hatred. It occurs on personal, institutional, and societal levels.

**Homosexual** A person who is physically, romantically, emotionally and/or spiritually attracted to a person of the same gender. Many prefer "gay," "lesbian," etc. because of the term's origins as a medical term at a time when homosexuality was considered a disorder.

**Homosexuality** A sexual orientation in which a person feels physically and emotionally attracted to people of the same gender.

**Inclusive language** The use of non-identity specific language to avoid imposing limitations or assumptions on others. For example, saying "you all" instead of "you guys" in order to not impose assumptions regarding a person's gender identity.

**In the closet** To be "in the closet" means to hide one's homosexual identity in order to keep a job, a housing situation, friends, or in some other way to survive. Many LGBT*⁺IAGCQQ individuals are "out" in some situations and "closeted" in others.

**Internalized homophobia** The fear and self-hate of one's own homosexuality or bisexuality that occurs for many individuals who have learned negative ideas about homosexuality throughout childhood. One form of internalized oppression is the acceptance of the myths and stereotypes applied to the oppressed group. Internalized oppression is commonly seen among most, if not all, minority groups.

**Intersex (IS)** Those born with atypical sex characteristics. A person whose natal physical sex is physically ambiguous. There are many genetic, hormonal, or anatomical variations which can cause this (e.g., Klinefelter syndrome, adrenal hyperplasia, or androgen insensitivity syndrome). Parents and medical professionals usually assign intersex infants a sex and perform surgical operations to conform the infant's body to that assignment, but this practice has become increasingly controversial as intersex adults are speaking out against having had to undergo medical procedures that they did not consent to (and in many cases caused them mental and physical difficulties later in life). The term intersex is preferred over "hermaphrodite," an outdated term which is stigmatizing and misleading.

**Invisibility** The constant assumption of heterosexuality renders gay and lesbian people, youth in particular, invisible and seemingly nonexistent. Gay and lesbian people and youth are usually not seen or portrayed in society, and especially not in schools and classrooms.

**Label free** Individuals who shirk all labels attached to gender and reject the gender binary.

**Latinx** A gender-neutral term for people of Latin American descent; possessing an identity outside of the female/male binary.

**Latin@** An unpronounceable gender-neutral shorthand for *Latino/Latina*.

**Lesbian** A feminine-identified individual who is emotionally, physically, romantically, sexually, and/or spiritually attracted to feminine-identified individuals.

**Monosexual/Multisexual** Umbrella terms for orientations directed towards one's gender (monosexual) or many genders (multisexual).

**Nonbinary gender identity** The expression of gender identity that does not fit any categorization or is not necessarily discernable to another. This expression can refuse, align with, or play with representations of gender, but doesn't have to shift over time and in context.

**Pansexual/Omnisexual** "Pan," meaning "all." Someone who is emotionally, physically, romantically, sexually, and/or spiritually attracted to all gender identities/expressions, including those outside the gender-conforming binary. Similar to bisexual, but different in that the concept deliberately rejects the gender binary. Polysexual people are attracted to "many," but not necessarily all, genders.

**Passing** A term used by transgender people to mean that they are seen as the gender with which they self-identify. For example, a transgender man (born female) who most people see as a man. Also a term used by non-heterosexual people to mean that they are seen as or assumed to be heterosexual.

**Polyamory** Having more than one intimate relationship at a time with the knowledge and consent of everyone involved. It is distinct from both swinging (which emphasizes sex with others as merely recreational) and polysexuality (which is attraction towards multiple genders and/or sexes). People who identify as polyamorous typically reject the view that sexual and relational exclusivity are necessary for deep, committed, long-term loving relationships.

**Preferred or claimed gender pronouns** Self-selected pronouns for how an individual prefers to be referenced. While there is an emerging lexicon of pronouns, it is best to ask the individual how one self-references.

**QPOC** Queer People Of Color or Queer Person Of Color.

**Queer** Despite the negative historical use of this term, it has been embraced in the last decade, particularly by younger members of the LGBT*⁺IAGCQQ community. It is an umbrella term that many prefer, both because of convenience (easier than "gay," "lesbian," etc.) and because it does not force the person who uses it to choose a more specific label for their gender identity or sexual orientation. Queer also refers to a suspension of rigid gendered and sexual orientation categories and is underscored by attempts to interrogate and interrupt heteronormativity, reinforced by acknowledging diverse people across gender, sex, and desire spectra, as well as to foreground the sexual. It embraces the freedom to move beyond, between, or even away from, yet even to later return to, myriad identity categories. Queer is not confined to LGBT*IAGCQ people, but is inclusive of any variety of experience that transcends what has been socially and politically accepted as normative categories for gender and sexual orientation.

**Queer autonomy or (a)gender and (a)sexual justice** These interchangeable terms each ideologically reflect the actualized freedom of humans to be self-expressive without fear of social, institutional, or political violence. See also *(a)gender and (a)sexual justice*.

**Romantic orientation** A person's enduring emotional, physical, romantic and/or spiritual—but not necessarily sexual—attraction to others. Sometimes called affectional orientation. "Romantic orientation" is often used by the asexual community in lieu of "sexual orientation."

**Safe space** A place where people who identify within the LGBT*IAGCQ communities feel comfortable and secure in being who they are. In this place, they can talk about the people with whom they are involved without fear of being criticized, judged, or ridiculed. Safe spaces promote the right to be comfortable in one's living space, work environments, etc. It is focused toward the right to use the pronoun of a significant other in conversation, and the right to be as outwardly open about one's life and activities as anyone else.

**Same-gender loving** A term created by the African-American community that some prefer to use instead of "lesbian," "bisexual," or "gay" to express attraction to and love of people of the same gender. SGL is an alternative to Eurocentric homosexual identities, which may not culturally affirm or engage the history and cultures of people of African descent.

**Self-determined** presumes the right to make choices to self-identify in a way that authenticates one's self-expression and self-acceptance, rejects an imposition to be externally controlled, defined, or regulated, and can unsettle knowledge to generate new possibilities of legibility.

**Sex** refers to the biological traits, which include internal and external reproductive anatomy, chromosomes, hormones, and other physiological characteristics. The assignment and classification of people at birth as male or female is often based solely on external reproductive anatomy. Related terms: intersex, female, male.

**Sexual orientation** A person's emotional, physical, and sexual attraction and the expression of that attraction. Although a subject of debate, sexual orientation is probably one of the many characteristics that people are born with.

**Sexual minority** A term used to refer to someone who identifies their sexuality as different from the dominant culture (i.e., heterosexual), for example, homosexual, gay, lesbian, bisexual, transsexual, transgender, or transvestite.

**Sexual affirmation/alignment/confirmation surgery** Establishing one's affirmed sex via legal and medical steps.

**Stealth** Going stealth means for a trans* person to live completely as their gender identity and to pass in the public sphere; when a trans* person chooses not to disclose their trans* status to others. This can be done for numerous reasons including safety, or simply because the person doesn't feel others have the right to know. For transsexuals, going stealth is often the goal of transition.

**Trans˙⁺** Trans*⁺ is technically synonymous with, though etymologically different from trans, trans*, and transgender. It is the experience of having a gender identity that is different from one's biological sex, or identify outside of the binary altogether. A trans*⁺ (trans, trans*, and transgender) person may be pre- or post-operative and is not defined by any predetermined or essentialized gender formula. This term has become an umbrella term for nonconforming gender identity and expression. Trans*⁺ when written with an asterisk and superscript plus sign, denotes transgender identities that continue to emerge as indeterminate. Trans* with only an asterisk denotes a segment of the transgender population that was inclusive of only some trans people's identities, while excluding others. *Trans* is a prefix or adjective used as an abbreviation of transgender, derived from the Greek word meaning "across from" or "on the other side of." Many consider trans to be an inclusive and useful umbrella term. When the prefix as affixed to gender it signifies all non-cisgender gender identities and a recognition of difference from cisgender people.

**Transgender (TG)** The experience of having a gender identity that is different from one's biological sex. A transgender person may identify with the opposite biological gender and want to be a person of that gender. A transgender person may or may not be pre-or post-operative; if they are, they are likely to refer to him/herself as transsexual. This has become an umbrella term for nonconforming gender identity and expression.

**Transmisogyny** This is the hatred of women or those who are feminine-identified, the expression of the feminine, or those who are feminine-of-center but not assigned female at birth.

**Transphobia** Irrational fear of trans* people through active prejudice and active discrimination by institutions, communities, and/or individuals that diminishes access to resources throughout mainstream society.

**Transition** Adopting one's affirmed, non-biological gender permanently. The complex process of leaving behind one's coercively assigned birth sex. Transition can include: coming out to one's family, friends, and/or co-workers; changing one's name and/or sex on legal documents; hormone therapy; and possibly (though not always) some form of surgery. It's best not to assume that someone will "complete" this process at any particular time: an individual's transition is finished when they are finally comfortable with how their gender identity is aligned with their body, and may not include going through all of the aforementioned steps.

**Trans* woman or Trans* man** Informal descriptors used relative to one's affirmed gender. Variants include T*, trans person, and trans folk.

**Transsexual people (TS)** Typically those taking all available medical and legal steps to transition from their assigned sex to their affirmed sex. Transitioning across the sexual binary can go from female to male (FTM) or male to female (MTF). Some go stealth, hiding their transsexual history.

**Two-spirit** A contemporary term that references historical multiple gender traditions in many First Nations cultures. These individuals were sometimes viewed in certain tribes as having two spirits occupying one body; two-spirit indicates a person whose body simultaneously manifests both a masculine and a feminine spirit. Many Native/First Nations people who are LGBT*IAGCQ or gender non-conforming identify as two-spirit; in many Nations, being two-spirit carries both great respect and additional commitments and responsibilities to one's community.

---

## When discussing or having conversations with people, it is best to avoid:

- She-male, tranny, transie, sex change, he-she, shim
- Sexual preference (suggests choice)
- Hermaphrodite (an outdated clinical term)

# Appendix H

## Trans*+ing Schools Checklist

| Priorities | Actions to be Taken (how can I meet the priority?) | Target Date |
| --- | --- | --- |
| Develop more self-awareness | | |
| Change/expand curriculum | | |
| Observe how signs and posters reinforce gender and gender-identity norms and change them | | |
| Approach language around identities expansively | | |
| Reframe the notion of refusal | | |
| Strive to approach schools as trans-sectional | | |
| Develop lessons that mediate internal safety | | |
| Shift the classroom environment to create external safety | | |
| Revisit classroom or school code of conduct | | |
| Work with colleagues on bathroom policies | | |
| Revisit the name of the GSA and consider how to make it more inclusive | | |
| Work with colleagues on sports policies relative to trans*+ and gender identity concerns | | |
| Revise all school forms *(be sure not to put a category that says "other," because those with complex gender identities are already othered—consider using "specify" for everyone)* | | |
| Create a school-wide, district-wide task force/focus group to address gender identity and trans*+ harassment (e.g., enumerating bullying policies, physical education classes) | | |

| Priorities | Actions to be Taken (how can I meet the priority?) | Target Date |
|---|---|---|
| Intervene when any student is bullied | | |
| Deepen community involvement about trans*+ and gender identity topics (your Pride Center) | | |
| Work with parents about gender identity and trans*+ topics | | |
| Work with school board members about gender identity and trans*+ issues | | |
| Draw from city, state, and national resources to support teaching | | |
| Stay appraised of city, state, and national policies that impact those with complex gender identities and trans*+ people and discuss them with students, colleagues, parents, etc., | | |
| Work with school health care workers about trans*+ etiquette and support | | |
| Work with school counselors about supporting students who are trans*+ and have complex gender identities | | |
| Work closely with administrators and leading experts to develop professional development models that can support all stakeholders in their ongoing awareness (challenge how cisgender assumptions and privileges can be disrupted and shifted) | | |
| Caucus state legislatures to change state policy about trans*+ and gender non-conforming/ binary rights to be more inclusive of health care needs, identification changes, and bullying policies. | | |

# Appendix I

## *Commitments* Toward Enacting Trans*+ and Gender Identity Safety and Inclusion

**Commitment #1:** Invest emotionally in the well-being of students and their right to exist in educational contexts without harassment for gender presentation. **Ask:** In what ways are students harmed? What should be changed?

- Look closely at how codes of conduct, forms, bathrooms, locker rooms, physical education classes, extracurricular participation regulations (especially in athletics), counseling and mental health supports, and language use and terminology attend to the needs of, and reflects the existence of, a continuum of gender identities.
  - *For example: In all areas noted above, ensure that all students' gender identities will be supported, recognized, and valued in our educational context.*

- Ensure that professional development prepares teachers, administrators, staff and other personnel to use language and terminology that reflects a continuum of gender identities.
  - *For example: Ask students how they want to be called on or referred to.*

- Ensure that professional development prepares teachers, administrators, and curriculum specialists to include opportunities that mirror or expand awareness and respect regarding a continuum of gender identities.
  - *For example: Context-wide, strive to include texts, films, writing assignments, images, art/ists, media representations, trailblazers, political movements, histories, musicians, poets, key figures, etc. that reflect different representations of gender identities.*

- Create an ongoing focus group.
  - *For example: Have monthly meetings where stakeholders study a text, issue, visit a local community organization, or policy, and map out strategies that can support gender-identity inclusivity. Meeting sites should be rotated.*

*Commitment #2*: Carve out strategies to address the inclusion of a continuum of gender identities across the educational context..
*Ask*: What kinds of supports do our stakeholders need to effectively attend to this work?

- Survey and interview stakeholders about what they know, want to know, and how to apply knowledge to their contexts.
  - *For example: Questions can range from background knowledge related to gender identity. Findings can be used to generate professional development opportunities.*
- Ask stakeholders about experts they would like to learn from.
  - *For example: Invite in speakers, use films, videos, texts, attend conferences, etc., to support capacity building.*
- Ask stakeholders to consider conducting research with students and school/university programs to better understand life through their eyes.
  - *For example: Consider ways to bridge the gender identity divide and create action research projects that are built into the curriculum.*

- *Commitment #3: Plan for and map how to create new opportunities where new social relations can form.*
*Ask*: How is power built into the dynamics of gender identity and how can we shift those dynamics.

- In surveys, focus groups, professional development, etc., ask stakeholders to reflect on how their own gender identities maintain and sustain gender identity hierarches of power. Ask them how they have created harm and what they want to change.
  - *For example: Create opportunities to closely reflect (as a group and individually) about how gender-typical identities maintain and sustain gender-identity power dynamics. Facilitate conversations about neoliberalism and create a long-term plan to both study those effects and how to shift the academic environment.*
- Reflect on from where issues about gender identity seem to spring.
  - *For example: Look closely at the spaces where bias exists and attend to those. Ask, do certain students cluster in only some classrooms? Is there a Gay Straight or Queer and Sexuality Alliance and who attends those meetings? Ask, do we need to rename the club to be more expansive? How can we bring students and teachers together so our environment is safe for everyone? Put up posters, signs, billboards, art,*

*rearrange classrooms, include more books with diverse gender identity representations in classrooms and the library, invite in speakers, show movies or videos, and rename spaces so that all gender identities are recognized.*

- **Commitment #4:** *Plan for and map how to shift power dynamics around allocations of social space, curriculum, and innovations.*
**Ask:** How do we navigate this work from the ground up?

- Take a group walk through the context and determine what spaces are funded more than others.
  - *For example: Assemble a group that examines and then creates a portfolio about how power operates and is sustained in the educational setting. Based on those findings, redistribute those resources (money, larger rooms, technology, etc.) that maintain power.*
- Examine how pedagogy and curriculum account for trans-sectionality.
  - *For example: Look closely at pedagogies that are monologic, authoritative, pedantic, and are not culturally responsive. Review how curriculum accounts for trans-sectional voices. Make changes that lead to more equity in the classroom.*
- Develop across-context models for assessing ongoing processes related to shifting dynamics of gender identity.
  - *For example: Create a long-term checks and balances plan to continually assess the distribution of finances.*
- Work closely with neighboring universities' teacher education programs
  - *For example: Have discussions about how to embed gender identity work across grade-level and disciplinary areas in preservice teacher education. Discuss lesson plans, pedagogy, and possibilities for research that can be co-created.*
- Review how spaces are liberatory.
  - *For example: How do social spaces reinforce dynamics of power about gender identity? Who holds power in that space? Collectively plan how to reframe the space so gender identities have equal representation.*

**Commitment #5:** Continually assess how changes are working, and invite stakeholders to help address and create forward-thinking solutions.
**Ask:** Have our strategies been effective in exposing or confronting the root causes that maintain the educational gender identity industrial complex? What do we need to do to build the educational system (world) we want to live in?

- Generate a list of reflections that address awareness now about root causes of gender identity subjugation.
  - *For example: With the list, compile a survey and distribute. Reflect on the findings and build those findings into continued efforts.*
- Reflect on what the environment should look like and construct a plan for wants and needs that will galvanize its realization.
  - *For example: Create working groups that attend to each of the identified areas and put a plan into motion with action steps and timelines that will help achieve the desired outcomes.*
- Reflect if root approaches to work are trans-sectional.
  - *For example: Evaluate how students' trans-secting identities frame the core of discussions. Be sure to disaggregate any data to see where disproportionality is situated. Make changes based on those findings.*
- Create resource packets to distribute to new stakeholders.
  - *For example: Create googledocs that support gender identity inclusivity in curricula, policies, resources, spaces, etc., for on-going use.*
- Assess that the work is process-oriented rather than end-oriented.
  - *For example: Ensure that all efforts reflect a continuum of gender identity inclusivity and the indeterminate for self-identification. This means staying open and aware to what may still come and being open to the work that will continue to support elasticity.*
- Continually cultivate new leaders who have the vision to challenge and change the system.
  - *For example: Create a strategic action plan that addresses the kinds of leadership styles and vested interest can be manifested in the educational context. Work to ensure that those styles and interests are present.*
- Determine strategies for school/university-wide and individual accountability.
  - *For example: Revisit the mission and vision statements. Create an equity profile that assesses how these criteria are implemented and demonstrate changes over time (e.g., informal, formative, summative). Make changes to the work as needed.*
- Develop a state-wide network dedicated to working with legislatures who can create policies and policy changes.

- *For example: Map out the policies and policy changes for your school/ university related but not to limited to athletics, enumeration in bullying laws, dress, bathroom, and locker room access, mental and physical health care, body safety, disciplinary practices (e.g., zero tolerance policies and overuse of subjective discipline infraction categories), identification rights, etc., and have ongoing discussions and meetings.*

# Appendix J

## Documentaries about transgender and gender non-binary individuals

**Film title:** *The Death and Life of Marsha P. Johnson*
**Where to view:** https://www.netflix.com/title/80189623
*The Death and Life of Marsha P. Johnson* is a feature-length documentary about the mysterious death of one of the most important activists in the movement for trans liberation.
**Length:** 105 minutes

**Film title:** *Diagnosing Difference*
**Where to view:** http://www.diagnosingdifference.com/
*Diagnosing Difference* is a feature-length length documentary featuring interviews with thirteen diverse scholars, activists, and artists who identify on the trans spectrum (transgender, transsexual, genderqueer, and gender variant) about the impact and implications of the Gender Identity Disorder (GID) on their lives and communities.
**Length:** 64 minutes

**Film title:** *The Family Journey: Raising Gender Nonconforming Children*
**Where to view:** http://www.youthandgendermediaproject.org/The_Family_Journey.html
*The Family Journey: Raising Gender Nonconforming Children* charts the emotional and intellectual transformations parents and siblings must make in order to successfully nurture their gender nonconforming family members. In frank, vulnerable interviews, families from all over the country speak about the power of love and acceptance to help their unusual children thrive. They also come to realize that loving a gender nonconforming child, in the face of ignorance—and sometimes—hostility, has turned them into more compassionate human beings.
**Length:** 14 minutes

**Film title:** *Gender Matters*
**Where to view:** http://cart.frameline.org/ProductDetails.asp?ProductCode
=T780
*Gender Matters* is six short films about transgender and gender non-conforming young adults.
**Length:** 74 minutes

**Film title:** *Gender Revolution*
**Where to view:** http://channel.nationalgeographic.com/gender-revolution-a-journey-with-katie-couric/
*Gender Revolution* follows Katie Couric as she sets out to explore the rapidly evolving complexities of gender identity.
**Length:** 133 minutes

**Film title:** *Gender: The Space Between*
**Where to view:** http://www.cbsnews.com/videos/gender-the-space-between/
*Gender: The Space Between* follows several youth and college students through their experiences coming to terms with their gender identities.
**Length:** 30 minutes
Two additional pieces break down the above documentary:

- *Role of Education, Parenting and Community on Gender Identity.*
  http://www.cbsnews.com/videos/the-role-of-education-parenting-and-community-in-gender-identity/
- *Breaking Down the Policy and Science Behind Gender Identity.* Interview by
  A. Wagner. CBS News
  http://www.cbsnews.com/videos/breaking-down-the-policy-science-behind-gender-identity/

**Film title:** *Growing Up Trans*
**Where to view:** http://www.pbs.org/wgbh/pages/frontline/growing-up-trans/
*Growing Up Trans* is a PBS Frontline Documentary that takes an intimate look at the struggles and choices facing transgender kids and their families.
**Length:** 84 minutes

**Film title:** *I'm Just Anneke*
**Where to view:** http://www.mediathatmattersfest.org/watch/10/im_just_anneke

*I'm Just Anneke* is the first film in a four-part series of short films called **The Youth and Gender Media Project** designed to educate school communities about transgender and gender nonconforming youth. The films are being used in schools and conferences throughout the US to train administrators, teachers, and students about the importance of protecting all children from harassment due to gender identity and expression.

**Length:** 11 minutes

**Film title:** *It Gets Messy in Here*
**Where to view:** http://www.youtube.com/watch?v=tis4k7zqDT4
*It Gets Messy in Here* is a short documentary challenging gender assumptions and gender identities of all kinds by delving into the bathroom experiences of masculine-identified queer women and transgender men of color, featuring performance artist D'Lo, Alice Y. Hom, Prentis Hemphill, Megan Benton, Dr. C. RIley Snorton, Jun-Fung Chueh-Mejia, jay-Marie Hill, and Che.

**Length:** 30 minutes

**Film title:** *Just Call Me Kade*
**Where to view:** http://www.youtube.com/watch?v=4pRt9pxmP0s
*Just Call Me Kade* follows Kade Farlow Collins who is a sixteen year old FTM (female to male transgender person) residing in Tucson, Arizona. Kade's parents maintain a supportive and nurturing relationship to Kade regarding the many challenges facing their teenage child. However, it hasn't always been easy.

**Length:** 26 minutes

**Film title:** *Limina*
**Where to View:** Turbid Lake Pictures: http://turbidlakepictures.com/projects/
*Limina* is about an intuitive gender-fluid child on a journey of kindness to change the lives of fellow townspeople in a picturesque village.

**Length:** 14 minutes

**Film title:** *Passing*
**Where to view:** https://www.amazon.com/Passing-Victor Thomas/dp/B01GEVQH0K/ref=sr_1_1_dvt_1_wnzw?s=instant-video&ie=UTF8&qid=1481061427&sr=1-1&keywords=passing

*Passing* is a short documentary profiling the lives of three men of color who have undergone gender transition from female to male. The film explores what life is like living as a black man, when no one knows you are transgender. This award-winning film is one of the few films to address the intersectionality of race, gender, and the experiences of those who walk multiple paths in life.
**Length:** 23 minutes

**Film title: *PBS First Person***
**Where to view:** http://www.pbs.org/show/first-person/
*PBS First Person* follows a number of different narratives of young adults about their different expressions of identity including intersectionality, queer of color, disability, intersex, non-binary, and being religious, to name a few. The site also features resources for teachers with tools for language, and connections to the standards.
**Length:** 6–7 minutes, varying in length

**Film title: *Pink Boy***
**Where to View:** PBS, POV: http://www.pbs.org/pov/pinkboy/video/pink-boy/
*Pink Boy* is an intimate portrait of a young transgender child in rural Florida at the moment of transition. Butch lesbian BJ successfully avoided wearing dresses her entire life. Then she and her partner, Sherrie, adopted Jeffrey, who, to their shock, started to dance in gowns and perform for his parents. As Jeffrey, now six, increasingly wishes to dress up in public, BJ must navigate where is safe, from school to a rodeo in Georgia to the ultimate holiday, for a "pink boy." Since filming ended, Jeffrey has transitioned and now identifies as a girl, Jessie, full-time. In 2015, *Pink Boy* won a Grand Jury Prize in the Shorts Competition of DOC NYC, Best Documentary Short at the Palm Springs International ShortFest, and Audience Award for Best Short at the Nantucket Film Festival.
**Length:** 9 minutes

**Film title: *Raised Without Gender***
**Where to view:** https://www.youtube.com/watch?v=4sPj8HhbwHs
*Raised Without Gender* follows the day-to-day life of one gender non-conforming family living in Sweden. Mapa (mom and dad) Del LaGrace Volcano—who was born intersex—and their two children, five-year-old Mika and three-year-old Nico share their experience of navigating their lives without the restrictions of gender.

**Length:** 29 minutes

**Film title:** *Real Boy*
**Where to view:** http://www.pbs.org/independentlens/films/real-boy/
*Real Boy* is an intimate story of a family in transition. As nineteen-year-old Bennett Wallace navigates early sobriety, late adolescence, and the evolution of his gender identity, his mother makes her own transformation from resistance to acceptance of her trans son. Along the way, both mother and son find support in their communities, reminding us that families are not only given, but chosen.
**Length:** varies by video, 72 minutes

**Film title:** *Screaming Queens*
**Where to view:** http://cart.frameline.org/ProductDetails.asp?ProductCode=T636
*Screaming Queens* tells the little-known story of the first known act of collective, violent resistance to the social oppression of queer people in the United States—a 1966 riot in San Francisco's impoverished Tenderloin neighborhood, three years before the famous gay riot at New York's Stonewall Inn.
**Length:** 57 minutes

**Film title:** *Straightlaced: How Gender's Got us All Tied Up*
**Where to view:** http://groundspark.org/our-films-and-campaigns/straightlaced
*Straightlaced* includes the perspectives of teens who self-identify as straight, lesbian, gay, bisexual, or questioning and represent all points of the gender spectrum. With courage and unexpected humor, they open up their lives to the camera: choosing between "male" and "female" deodorant; deciding whether to go along with anti-gay taunts in the locker room; having the courage to take ballet; avoiding the restroom so they won't get beaten up; or mourning the suicide of a classmate. It quickly becomes clear that just about everything teens do requires thinking about gender and sexuality.
**Length:** 67 minutes

**Film title:** *This is Me*
**Where to view:** https://www.amazon.com/This-Is-Me/dp/B010BYPAYA
*This is Me*, a docu-series, is an anthology of five 3–5 minute-long *Transparent*-inspired documentaries by five different trans and gender-nonconforming

filmmakers. Personal essays, direct actions, explainers—each filmmaker has crafted a segment that explores a theme in *Transparent.*
**Length:** five documentaries, 4–6 minutes long

**Film title:** *The Trans List*
**Where to view:** http://www.hbo.com/documentaries/the-trans-list
*The Trans List* is a documentary that features interviews and an introduction by Janet Mock. It features such outspoken subjects as Kylar Broadus, Caroline Cossey, Amos Mac, Bamby Salcedo, Buck Angel, Miss Major Griffin-Gracy, Nicole Maines, Shane Ortega, Caitlyn Jenner, Alok Vaid-Menon, and Laverne Cox, sharing their stories in their own words, addressing identity, family, career, love, struggle, and accomplishment.
**Length:** 57 minutes

**Film title:** *TRANSFORMATION*
**Where to view:** https://www.youtube.com/watch?v=qA5fNBQNVyE or, http://www.mtv.com/shows/transformation
*MTV's TRANSFORMATION* is a documentary about a group of transgender teens and young adults struggling to find the resources, safety, and confidence to express their gender identity. With 45 percent of young transgender people having reportedly attempted suicide in the United States alone, non-binary stylist Madin Lopez has made it their business to provide life-altering, gender-affirming makeovers. Afterwards, these individuals are hopefully able to be their true and best selves, looking on the outside how they've always felt on the inside.
**Length:** 45 minutes

**Film title:** *Transgender Basics*
**Where to view:** http://www.gaycenter.org/gip/transbasics/video
*Transgender Basics* is a 20-minute educational film on the concepts of gender and transgender people. Two providers from the Gender Identity Project discuss basic concepts of gender—sex, identity, and gender roles—as three transgender community members share their personal experiences of being trans and genderqueer. The film targets service providers and others working with the LGBT community, but it also provides a fascinating glimpse into gender and identity for the general public.
**Length:** 19 minutes

**Film title:** *Treasure: From Tragedy to TransJustice: Mapping a Detroit Story*
**Where to view:** http://www.treasuredoc.com
*Treasure* is a feature-length, award-winning documentary about nineteen year old transwoman Shelly "Treasure" Hilliard whose murder involved police coercion, Jim Crow drug laws, the criminalization of sex work, and transphobia. It is about a young Detroit trans community activated by her death, and her family, who are suing for justice.
**Length:** 63 minutes

**Film title:** *TRUTH—Share Your Story*
**Where to view:** https://transgenderlawcenter.org/programs/truth/truth-share-your-story
*TRUTH—Share Your Story,* housed on the Transgender Law Center website, is a space for youth to share their stories and have them archived in narrative or in video.
**Length:** varies by video, 2–5 minutes

**Film title:** *We've Been Around*
**Where to view:** https://www.youtube.com/playlist?list=PLfNvZrTLs1tVmwno BD3UIEGOyV4hZljF-
*We've Been Around,* created by Rhys Ernst (co-producer of Amazon's hit *Transparent*) and produced by Christine Beebe, is a series of documentary shorts that chronicle the lives of Lucy Hicks Anderson, STAR, Albert, Little Axe, Lou Sullivan, and Camp TRANS.
**Length:** six documentaries, 4–5 minutes long

**Film title:** *Where We Are Now*
**Where to view:** https://www.youtube.com/watch?v=dYmLLhK3Kw4
*Where We Are now,* made by Scottish artist filmmaker Lucie Rachel, is an insightful personal documentary about the relationship between a young bisexual woman and her transgender parent, who recently made the decision to transition. The moving film presents viewers a rare, intimate look at a non-heteronormative family. The film pairs clips of Rachel and her parent going about their daily lives with candid voiceover reflections on the transition process. *Where We Are Now* shines as a testament to the simple truth that we are all more similar than we are different. It was named "Best Scottish Short" at the Scottish Queer International Film Festival and won "Best Documentary" at the Forbes Under 30 Film Festival.
**Length:** 9 minutes

# Appendix K

## Classroom/School Scenarios

*Read your scenario and discuss.*

**I.** A student/colleague/supervisor/or staff member in your (fill in context) _____ presents as gender fluid/ambiguous/creative/expansive/dynamic and you realize that you have failed to address a spectrum of how gender is represented in your classrooms or district and through your policies. How do you approach this topic without drawing attention to the student?

**II.** A student/colleague/supervisor/or staff in in your (fill in context) _____ tells you that they do not use pronouns and is (a)gender. In that moment, you recognize that you have not opened your (fill in context) _____ in ways that make others feel comfortable disclosing their claimed names/identities/pronouns. How do you approach this topic?

**III.** A student/colleague/supervisor/or staff member in your (fill in context) _____ tells you that they are being bullied for being trans*+ or gender nonbinary. In that moment, you recognize that while you have addressed some forms of bullying that you have not addressed trans*+ and gender-identity-complex microaggressions. How do you approach this topic?

**IV.** A group of queer students of color approach you in (fill in context) _____ and tell you that no curricula, books, movies, art, or even discussions reflect their trans-sectional identities but that their peers are clearly recognized in the classroom, school, or district. How do you approach this?

**V.** You have a deep "AHA" moment one night while listening to NPR's Radiolab. You realize that educational contexts are driven far more by neoliberal values and principles than in times past. Pining for what once was, you tell yourself that all students deserve equitable schooling opportunities and deserve to be valued for who they are. How can you bring in a discussion to your (fill in context) _____ about how neoliberalism perpetuates systemic oppressions that "reinforce and sustain compulsory heterosexism, and cissexism which secure homophobia, and cissexualism; and how gendering and a cisgender assumption secure bullying and transphobia."

**VI.** A colleague, supervisor, staff member, or student tells you that gender is fixed, stable, and never changes. How do you respond? How do you offer a different perspective without negating their beliefs?

**VII.** On your first day of work at (fill in context) _____ you make regrettable assumptions about someone else's gender and identity and call them **he** or **she** based on how they look. After a professional development session, a trans*+ and/or gender identity nonbinary colleague, supervisor, and/or staff member comes up to you and says that they do not use pronouns and is/are (a) gender. How do you respond?

**VIII.** A student/colleague/professor, or staff member in your (fill in context) _____ tells you that they do not believe in gender and that femininity and masculinity are both constructed. You appreciate their insights and decide to make it into a learning unit. Tell us what you do!

**IX.** Drawing on the Supreme Court case of Gavin Grimm and the right to use a bathroom that matches his gender identity, what can you do to generate or further discussions about transgender and gender non-conforming students' rights and protections in your educational context?

**X.** In your educational context, when you speak about people's sex you consistently identify them as male and female. Unbeknownst to you, you have a colleague/student/supervisor/or staff member who is intersex but you have never brought intersex topics into focus in any of your work. One day they approach you and disclose their true identity. How do you respond and how do you begin to include intersex discussions in your work without relying on them to be your teacher?

**XI.** Please invent a scenario relative to your context.

# Appendix L

## Risks and Resources

### Gender Diversity

Gender is a fundamental aspect of identity and is often (erroneously) viewed as a binary concept with two fixed and mutually exclusive options, male or female, which are grounded in a person's physical anatomy (Murchison, 2016; Pyne, 2012; Simons, Leibowitz, and Hidalgo, 2014). Beneath this dualistic, reductive conceptualization of gender lies a far more complex, diverse, and rich reality (Malpas, 2011; Simons et al., 2014). Indeed, anthropological, historical, social, and biological data reveal that an individual's sense of gender is more accurately understood as an interweaving of biology, environment, and culture (Ehrensaft, 2011; 2016). As such, the construct of gender diversity provides a more nuanced and accurate model of human gender.

The notion of gender diversity is increasingly seen as an important way for schools, families, organizations, and society to reflect the heterogeneity of students who do not conform to social gender expectations, and it has been argued that the concept of gender diversity thus must inform best practices in supports for transgender, gender creative, and gender-conforming youth alike (Olson, 2015; Wells, Roberts, and Allan, 2012).

## Risk Factors for Transgender and Gender Diverse Youth

Transgender and gender diverse youth are at high risk for a number of negative academic, social, and health outcomes (Greytak, Kosciw, and Diaz, 2009; Meyer, Taylor, and Peter, 2015; Toomey, Ryan, Diaz, Card, and Russell, 2010). They often face high levels of social stressors and risk factors in school settings, including: academic difficulties; social exclusion, bullying, and violence; family rejection; mental health concerns; and suicide (Veale et al., 2015; Wells, Frohard-Dourlent, Saewyc, Ferguson, and Veale, 2017). There is an ironic and concerning parallel between the stereotyped and tragic representations of trans people in media and in research. Indeed, many trans youth can deftly rattle off statistics about these significant and disproportionate risks, and over a decade of methodologically sound research indicates that they are thoroughly correct, as summarized below.[1]

Gender diverse youth experience high levels of risk for academic difficulties such as learning problems, absenteeism, and dropping out (Wells et al., 2012; Veale et al, 2015). They experience disproportionately hostile school environments, hear biased language, feel unsafe in school, are regularly harassed, and lack resources and supports (Grant et al., 2011; Greytak et al., 2009). Transgender and gender diverse students experience higher rates of peer victimization, including verbal teasing, social rejection, and physical aggression than their gender-conforming peers (Grossman and D'Augelli, 2006; Taylor et al., 2011; Toomey et al., 2010). Many gender diverse students also experience rejection, discrimination, and violence in their families due to their gender expression (Veale et al., 2015); highly rejecting family behaviours are strongly correlated with negative mental and physical health outcomes. Along these lines, trans students experience increased risk for a number of negative mental health outcomes, including anxiety, depression, suicidality, oppositional defiance, self-injury, and substance abuse (Veale et al., 2015). Such mental health difficulties typically emanate from minority stress, defined as "the excess stress to which individuals from stigmatized groups are exposed as a result of their social, often a minority, position" (Meyer, 2003, p. 3), rather than from gender diversity itself (Olson, Durwood, DeMeules, and McLaughlin, 2015; Pyne, 2012; Veale et al., 2015). And perhaps the most alarming and most reported risk factor for transgender and gender nonconforming students remains suicidal ideation, attempts, and completions (Bauer, Scheim, Pyne, Travers, and Hammond, 2015; Grossman and D'Augelli, 2007; Stieglitz, 2010). Certainly, suicide risk for trans youth represents an urgent health crisis that requires immediate attention in schools, families, and communities (Wells et al., 2017).

# Support and Resources

- *The Gender Identity Workbook for Children* by Kelly Storck
- *Trans Student Education Resource*, http://www.transstudent.org/
- *GLSEN Report*, https://www.glsen.org/

- *Alberta Teachers' Association Prism Toolkit*, Secondary Edition https://www.teachers.ab.ca/SiteCollectionDocuments/ATA/Publications/Research/PD-80-15e%20PRISM.pdf
- *Supporting and Caring for Transgender Children*, http://hrc-assets.s3-website-us-east-1.amazonaws.com//files/documents/SupportingCaringforTransChildren.pdf
- *Gender Spectrum*, http://www.genderspectrum.org/
- *Gender Creative Kids Canada*, http://gendercreativekids.ca/
- *GLAAD Media Reference Guide*, 10th Edition, https://www.glaad.org/reference
- *Families in TRANSition: A Resource Guide for Parents of Trans Youth*, https://www.rainbowhealthontario.ca/resources/families-in-transition-a-resource-guide-for-parents-of-trans-youth/

## Note

1   Skagerberg, Parkinson, and Carmichael (2013) note that although sexuality is distinct from gender identity, lesbian, gay, bisexual, transgender, and queer (LGBTQ) individuals often have gender nonconformity in common and, thus, comparisons are often made between these groups in the literature. As such, research involving LGBTQ samples is included in this review.

# Glossary of Shifting Terms

**(A)gender or agender** refers to the rejection of gender as a biological or social construct altogether and the refusal to identify with gender.

**(A)pronoun or apronoun** is an extension to the rejection of gender as a biological or social construct and thereby a refusal to use or be identified with or by a pronoun.

**Cisgender Gaze** refers to representations in which transgender and non-binary people are seen through the eyes of a cisgender person. The cisgender gaze can be voyeuristic, and cissexist in its normalization of a cisgender point of view.

**Cisgender/cis or Cissexual** is a person who by nature or by choice conforms to gender-based expectations of society. Cisgender individuals have a gender identity that tends to be aligned with their birth sex, and thereby tend to have a self-perception and gender expression that matches behaviors and roles considered appropriate for their birth sex. Cisgender people are also on a continuum of gender identities and there is no one way that a cisgender person *must* be. It is important to recognize that even if two people identify as men (one being cis and the other being trans*+), they may lead very similar lives but deal with different struggles pertaining to their birth sex. The prefix "cis" is of Latin origin, meaning "on the same side (as)" and evolved from the use of the term "transgender" as a recognition and signifier that there are different types of gender identities.

**Cisgender Assumption** is the condition of and practice of reinforcing cisgender privilege, cisnormativity, and the cisgender/cissexual body, unknowingly or with intention, and contributes to the marginalization and erasure of complex gender identities.

**Cisheteropatriarchy** refers to social systems in which cisgender, heterosexual men hold power. This term originated from the concept of patriarchy, but has evolved to include dimensions of cissexism and heterosexism.

**Cissexualism and Cissexism** is the impact of the cisgender assumption that all gender-normative-appearing bodies are always not trans*+.

**Cisnormativity** refers to the assumption that individuals are cisgender.

**Cisgender Privilege** is the unquestionable entitlement and the tendency to move throughout life without the experience or fear of ill treatment because of one's body, and the congruity between how a person looks, acts, and behaves in accordance with how the perceiver reads the perceived.

**Gender Identity Complexity** is the constant integration of new ideas and concepts and the invention of new knowledges—comprised of multitudes, and/or, a moving away, or sometimes a refusal to accept essentialized constructions of binaries, genders, and bodies. Yet, in simultaneity, gender identity can be some of these, all of these and none of these. It avoids the straightjacket of being categorized. Also written as *complex gender identity/identities, gender-identity complex* or the *complexity/complexities of gender identity/identities.*

**Gender Identity Self-Determination** is the state of, and right to, self-identify in a way that authenticates one's self-expression and self-acceptance, and which refuses to be externally controlled, defined, or regulated.

**Trans**\*+ is technically synonymous with, though etymologically different from trans, trans\*, and transgender. It is the experience of having a gender identity that is different from one's biological sex, or of identifying outside of the binary altogether. A trans\*+ (trans, trans\*, and transgender) person may be pre- or post-operative and is not defined by any predetermined or essentialized gender formula. This term has become an umbrella term for nonconforming gender identity and expression.

Trans\*+ when written with an asterisk and superscript plus sign, denotes transgender identities that continue to emerge as indeterminate. Trans\* with only an asterisk denotes a segment of the transgender population that was inclusive of only some trans people's identities, while excluding others. In my writing, I use the superscript plus sign + to symbolize the ever-expanding and indeterminate ways of self-identifying, and the asterisk to honor those who fought for gender identity self-determination, which paved way for new identities to emerge.

**"Trans"** is a prefix or adjective used as an abbreviation of transgender, derived from the Greek word meaning "across from" or "on the other side of." Many also consider "trans" to be an inclusive and useful umbrella term. When the prefix is affixed to gender it signifies all non-cisgender gender identities and a recognition of difference from cisgender people.

**Transface** is the controversial practice of cisgender performers portraying transgender characters. The term derives its origin from "blackface," a racist practice from Vaudeville and early cinema where White performers would use makeup to portray offensive and cartoonish versions of Black people.

**Transmisogyny** is the hatred of women or those who are feminine-identified, who make an expression of the feminine, or who are feminine-of-center but not assigned female at birth.

**Trans-sectionality** is a coming together of multiple forms of identities that are always in perpetual deconstruction and construction and are identified by their indeterminate integration and the ever-shifting amalgamation of identities. It is the generation and embedding of new knowledges and recognitions of self-awareness that both shakes up and wakes up contexts, and presumes that identities are unfixed yet stabilized by the act of self-determining one's gender identity.

# References

Aikenhead, D. (2018). RuPaul: "Drag is a big f-you to male-dominated culture." *The Guardian,* March 3. Available online: www.theguardian.com/tv-and-radio/2018/mar/03/rupaul-drag-race-big-f-you-to-male-dominated-culture.

Airton, L. (2013). Leave "those kids" alone: On the conflation of school homophobia and suffering queers. *Curriculum Inquiry* 43(5), 532–562.

Bauer, G. R., Hammond, R., Travers, R., Kaay, M., Hohenadel, K. M., and Boyce, M. (2009). "I don't think this is theoretical; this is our lives": How erasure impacts health care for transgender people. *Journal of the Association of Nurses in AIDS Care,* 20, 348–361.

Bauer, G. R., Scheim, A. I., Pyne, J., Travers, R., and Hammond, R. (2015). Intervenable factors associated with suicide risk in transgender persons: A respondent driven sampling study in Ontario, Canada. *BMC Public Health,* 15(1), 525. http://doi.org/10.1186/s12889-015-1867-2.

Beauchamp, T. (2018). Clutching on: Teaching identity and terminology in transgender studies. *Feminist Formations* 30(3), 25–33.

Beauvoir, Simone de. (1989) [1952]. *The second sex.* Translated by H. M. Parshley. New York, NY: Vintage Books/Random House.

Bell, C. (2018). How Greg Berlanti made the movie queer kids (and adults) have been waiting for: The director on "Love, Simon," his own closeted adolescence, and the importance of more LGBTQ+ representations in film. *MTV News.* Available online: www.mtv.com/news/3069577/love-simon-greg-berlanti-interview/.

Bettcher, T. M. (2006). Appearance, reality, and gender deception: Reflections on transphobic violence and the politics of pretence. In *Violence, Victims, Justifications: Philosophical Approaches,* edited by F. Murchadha. Oxford: Peter Lang.

Bettcher, T. M. (2013). "Evil deceivers and make-believers: On transphobic violence and the politics of illusion. In *The Transgender Studies Reader 2,* edited by Susan Stryker and Aren Z. Aizura, 278–290. New York: Routledge.

Bordo, S. (1993). *Unbearable Weight: Feminism, Western Culture and the Body.* Berkeley, CA: University of California Press.

Butler, J. (1988). Performative acts and gender constitution: An essay in phenomenology and feminist theory. In *Writing on the Body: Female Embodiment and Feminist Theory*, edited by K. Conboy, N. Medina, and S. Stanbury. New York, NY: Columbia University Press.

Dank, B. M. (1971). 'Coming out in the gay world'. *Psychiatry* 34, 180–197.

de Sousa, D. (2018). Trans representation is a matter of life and death. *The Hofstra Chronicle*, April 3. Available online: www.thehofstrachronicle.com/category/editorials/2018/4/3/trans-representation-is-matter-of-life-and-death.

Du Bois, W. E. B. (1903). *Souls of Black Folks*. Chicago: A.C.

Earl, J. (2018). Why is transface so offensive? Not sure why the recent Scarlett Johansson controversy has the trans community upset? Jessie Gender explains. *The Advocate*. Available online: www.advocate.com/transgender/2018/7/13/why-transface-so-offensive.

Earnest (2018). The demographics of video gaming. *Earnest*. Available online: www.earnest.com/blog/the-demographics-of-video-gaming/.

Ehrensaft, D. (2011). *Gender Born, Gender Made*. New York: The Experiment Publishing.

Ehrensaft, D. (2016). *The Gender Creative Child: Pathways for Nurturing and Supporting Children Who Live Outside Gender Boxes*. New York, NY: The Experiment Publishing.

Ellis, H. (1927). *Studies in the Psychology of Sex Volume II: Sexual Inversion*. 3rd Ed. Project Gutenberg.

Equality Federation (n.d.) About. Available online: www.equalityfederation.org/about/.

Farley, L. (2018). *Childhood Beyond Pathology: A Psychoanalytic Study of Development and Diagnosis*. Albany, NY: SUNY Press.

Fausto-Sterling, A. (1992). *Myths of Gender: Biological Theories About Women and Men*. New York, NY: Basic Books.

Fausto-Sterling, A. (2000). *Sexing the Body: Gender Politics and the Construction of Sexuality*. New York: Basic Books.

Fausto-Sterling, A. (2012). *Sex/Gender: Biology in a Social World*. New York, NY: Routledge Press.

Feinberg, L. (1992). *Transgender Liberation: A Movement Whose Time has Come*. New York, NY: World View Forum.

Feinberg, L. (1996). *Transgender Warriors: Making History from Joan of Arc to Dennis Rodman*. Boston: Beacon.

Foucault, M. (1978). *The History of Sexuality: An Introduction*. New York: Random House.

GLSEN (2016). *Educational Exclusion: Drop out, Push out, and School-to-Prison Pipeline among LGBTQ Youth*. New York: GLSEN.

Goffman, E. (1963). *Stigma: Notes on the Management of Spoiled Identity*. New York: Simon & Schuster.

Grant, J. M., Mottet, L. A, Tanis, J., Harrison, J., Herman, J. L., and Keisling, M. (2011). Injustice at every turn: A report of the national transgender discrimination survey. *Washington National Center for Transgender Equality and National Gay and Lesbian Task Force*, 25. http://doi.org/10.1016/S0016-7878(90)80026-2.

Green, J. (2004). *Becoming a Visible Man*. Nashville, TN: Vanderbilt University Press.

Greytak, E. A., Kosciw, J. G., and Diaz, E. M. (2009). *Harsh Realities: The Experiences of Transgender Youth in our Nation's School*. New York: GLSEN.

Grossman, A. H., and D'Augelli, A. R. (2006). Transgender youth: Invisible and vulnerable. *Journal of Homosexuality*, 51(1), 111–128.

Grossman, A. H., and D'Augelli, A. R. (2007). Transgender youth and life-threatening behaviors. *Suicide and Life-Threatening Behavior*, 37(5). http://doi.org/10.1521/suli.2007.37.5.527.

Halberstam, J. (1998). *Female Masculinity*. Durham, NC: Duke University Press.

Halberstam, J. (2018). *Trans*: A Quick and Quirky Account of Gender Variability*. Berkeley, CA: University of California Press.

Hardell, A. (2016). *ABCs of LGBT+*. Coral Gables, FL: Mango Publishing.

Harvard Law School (n.d.). Litigation: Impact. Available online: https://hls.harvard.edu/dept/opia/what-is-public-interest-law/public-interest-work-types/impact-litigation/#tab1-1.

Hatzenbuehler, M., Bellatorre, A., Lee, Y., Finch, B., Muenning, P., and Fiscella, K. (2014). Structural stigma and all cause mortality in sexual minority populations. *Social Science Medicine*, 103, 33–41.

Hatzenbuehler, M., McLaughlin, K., Keyes, K., and Hasin, D. (2010). The impact of institutional discrimination on psychiatric disorders in lesbian, gay, and bisexual populations: A prospective study. *American Journal of Public Health*, 100, 452–459.

Hendricks, M. L., and Testa, R. J. (2012). A conceptual framework for clinical work with transgender and gender nonconforming clients: An adaptation of the Minority Stress Model. *Professional Psychology: Research and Practice*, 43(5), 460–467.

Herman, J. L., Flores, A. R., Brown, T. N. T., Wilson, B. D. M., and Conron, K. J. (2017). *Age of Individuals Who Identify as Transgender in the United States*. Los Angeles, CA: Williams Institute, UCLA School of Law.

hooks, b. (1992). *Black Looks: Race and Representation*. Toronto, ON: Between the Lines.

Hoskin, R. A. (2013). Femme theory: Femininity's challenge to western feminist pedagogies. (Master's thesis). QSpace at Queen's University, Kingston, Ontario, Canada. https://qspace.library.queensu.ca/handle/1974/8271.

Hoskin, R. A. (2016). Westernization and the transmogrification of Sailor Moon. *InterAlia: A Journal of Queer Studies*, 13, 1–14.

Hoskin, R. A. (2017). Femme theory: Refocusing the intersectional lens. *Atlantis: Critical Studies in Gender, Culture & Social Justice*, 38(1), 95–109.

Hoskin, R. A. (2018a). Critical femininities: The development and application of Femme Theory. (dissertation). QSpace at Queen's University, Kingston, Ontario, Canada. https://qspace.library.queensu.ca/handle/1974/24491.

Hoskin, R. A. (2018b). Gender, health, and popular culture: Historical perspectives. *Atlantis: Critical Studies in Gender, Culture & Social Justice*, 39(1), 79–81.

Hoskin, R. A. (2019). Femmephobia: The role of anti-femininity and gender policing in LGBTQ+ people's experiences of discrimination. *Sex Roles*.

Human Rights Campaign. (2018). Violence against the transgender community. Available online: www.hrc.org/resources/violence-against-the-transgender-community-in-2018.

Hyde, J. S., Bigler, R. S., Joel, D., Tate, C. C., and van Anders, S. M. (2019). The future of sex and gender in psychology: Five challenges to the gender binary. *American Psychologist*, 74(2), 171–193.

*Island Trees Union Free School District No. 26, et al. v. Pico*, (1982). 457 US 853.

Jagose, A. (1996). *Queer Theory: An Introduction* (Reprint . ed.). New York, NY: New York University Press.

James, S. E., Brown, C., and Wilson, I. (2017). *2015 U.S. Transgender Survey: Report on the Experiences of Black Respondents*. Washington, DC and Dallas, TX: National Center for Transgender Equality, Black Trans Advocacy, & National Black Justice Coalition.

James, S. E. and Salcedo, B. (2017). *2015 U.S. Transgender Survey: Report on the Experiences of Latino/a Respondents*. Washington, DC and Los Angeles, CA: National Center for Transgender Equality and TransLatin@ Coalition.

Johnston, J. (2015). Understanding "Transgenderism." Available online: www.focusonthefamily.com/socialissues/sexuality/transgenderism/ understanding-transgenderism.

Kessler, S. (1998). *Lessons from the Intersexed*. New Brunswick, NJ: Rutgers University Press.

Kierski, W., and Blazina, C. (2009). The male fear of the feminine and its effects on counseling and psychotherapy. *The Journal of Men's Studies*, 17(2), 155–172.

King, T. (2003). *The Truth about Stories*. Toronto, ON: House of Anansi Press.

Kogan, T. (2017). Public restrooms and the distorting of transgender identity. *North Carolina Law Review*, 95, 1205–1239.

Kosciw, J. G., Greytak, E. A., Bartkiewicz, M. J., Boesen, M. J., and Palmer, N. A. (2012). *The 2011 National School Climate Survey: The Experiences of Lesbian, Gay, Bisexual and Transgender Youth in Our Nation's Schools*. New York: GLSEN.

Malpas, J. (2011). Between pink and blue: A multi-dimensional family approach to gender nonconforming children and their families. *Family Process*, 50(4), 453–470. http://doi.org/10.1111/j.1545-5300.2011.01371.x.

Mayo, C. (2017). Queer and trans youth, relational subjectivity, and uncertain possibilities: Challenging research in complicated contexts. *Educational Researcher*, 46(9), 530–538. DOI:10.3102/0013189X17738737.

Mbembe, A. (2003). Necropolitics. *Public Culture*, 15(1), 11–40.

Meadow, T. (2018). *Trans Kids: Being Gendered in the Twenty-First Century*. Berkeley, CA: University of California Press.

Meyer, E. J., Taylor, C., and Peter, T. (2015). Perspectives on gender and sexual diversity (GSD)-inclusive education: Comparisons between gay/lesbian/ bisexual and straight educators. *Sex Education*, 15(3), 221–234. http://doi. org/10.1080/14681811.2014.979341.

Meyer, I. H. (2003). Prejudice, social stress, and mental health in lesbian, gay, and bisexual populations: Conceptual issues and research evidence. *Psychololgical Bulletin*, 129(5), 674–697.

Miller, s. (2015a). Reading YAL queerly: A queer literacy framework for inviting (a)gender and (a)sexuality self-determination and justice. In *Beyond Borders: Queer Eros and Ethos (Ethics) in LGBTQ Young Adult Literature*, edited by D. Carlson and D. Linville, 153–180. New York, NY: Peter Lang.

Miller, s. (2015b). A queer literacy framework promoting (a)gender and (a) sexuality self- determination and justice. *English Journal*, 104(5), 37–44.

Miller, s. (ed.). (2016). *Teaching, Affirming, and Recognizing Trans and Gender Creative Youth: A queer Literacy Framework.* New York: PalgraveMacmillan.

Miller, s. (ed.). (2018a). Enseñando, afirmando, y reconociendo a jóvenes trans\* y de género creative: Un marco de enseñanza queer (A. Stevenson Valdés, Trans). Santiago: Ediciones Universidad Alberto Hurtado.

Miller, s. (2018b) Reframing schooling to liberate gender identity. *Multicultural Perspectives*, (20)2, 70–80.

Miller, s. (2019). *About gender identity justice in schools and communities.* New York, NY: Teachers College Press.

Miller, s., Mayo, C., and Lugg, C.A. (2018). Sex and gender in transition in US schools: Ways forward. *Sex Education*, 18, (4), 345–359, https://doi.org/10. 1080/14681811.2017.1415204.

Movement Advancement Project and GLSEN. (2017). Separation and stigma: Transgender youth & school facilities. Available online: http://lgbtmap.org/ transgender-youth-school.

Mulvey, L. (1975). Visual pleasure and narrative cinema. *Screen*, 16(3), 6–18. https://doi.org/10.1093/screen/16.3.6.

Mumford, L. (1934) [2010]. *Technics and Civilization.* Chicago, IL: University of Chicago Press.

Murchison, G. (2016). *Supporting & Caring for Transgender Children.* Washington, DC. Available online: http://hrc-assets.s3-website-us-east-1. amazonaws.com//files/documents/SupportingCaringforTransChildren.pdf.

Namaste, V. (2009). Undoing theory: The "transgender question" and the epistemic violence of Anglo-American feminist theory. *Hypatia*, 24, 11–32.

Olson, K. R., Durwood, L., DeMeules, M., and McLaughlin, K. A. (2015). Mental health of transgender children who are supported in their identities. *Pediatrics*, 137(3). http://doi.org/10.1542/peds.2015-3223.

Orr, A. and Baum, J. (2015). *Schools in Transition: A Guide for Supporting Transgender Students in K–12 Schools.* National Center for Lesbian Rights (NCLR) and Gender Spectrum.

Paris, D., and Alim, H. S. (2014). What are we seeking to sustain through culturally sustaining pedagogy? A loving critique forward. *Harvard Educational Review*, 84(1), 85–100.

Pyne, J. (2012). *Supporting Gender Independent Children.* Toronto: Rainbow Health Ontario.

Reynolds, D. (2015). Is "transface" a problem in Hollywood? *The Advocate.* Available online: www.advocate.com/arts-entertainment/2015/02/25/ transface-problem-hollywood.

Serano, J. (2007). *Whipping Girl: A Transsexual Woman on Sexism and the Scapegoating of Femininity*. Berkeley, CA: Seal Press.

Serano, J. (n.d.). *Trans-Misogyny Primer*. Available online: www.juliaserano. com/av/TransmisogynyPrimer-Serano.pdf.

Simons, L., Leibowitz, S. F., and Hidalgo, M. A. (2014). Understanding gender variance in children and adolescents. *Pediatric Annals*, 43(6), e126–e131. http://doi.org/10.3928/00904481-20140522-07.

Simons, L., Schrager, S. M., Clark, L. F., Belzer, M., and Olson, J. (2013). Parental support and mental health among transgender adolescents. *Journal of Adolescent Health*, 53(6), 791–793.

Skagerberg, E., Parkinson, R., and Carmichael, P. (2013). Self-harming thoughts and behaviors in a group of children and adolescents with gender dysphoria. *International Journal of Transgenderism*, 14, 86–92. http://doi.or g/10.1080/15532739.2013.817321.

Smith, G. A. (2017). 'Views of Transgender Issues Divide Along Religious Lines', Pew Research. Available online: www.pewresearch.org/fact-tank/2017/11/27/views-of-transgender-issues-divide-along-religious-lines/.

Stieglitz, K. A. (2010). Development, risk, and resilience of transgender youth. *Journal of the Association of Nurses in AIDS Care*, 21, 192–206. http://doi. org/10.1016/j.jana.2009.08.004.

Stryker, S. (2008). *Transgender History*. Cambridge, MA: De Capo Press.

Susset, F. (2014). Between a rock and a hard place: The experience of parents of gender non-conforming boys. In *Supporting Transgender and Gender Creative Youth*, edited by E. Meyer and A. Pullen Sansfaçon, 111–127. New York, NY: Peter Lang Publishing.

Taylor, C. and Peter, T., with McMinn, T. L., Elliott, T., Beldom, S., Ferry, A., Gross, Z., Paquin, S., and Schachter, K. (2011). *Every Class in Every School: The First National Climate Survey on Homophobia, Biphobia, and Transphobia in Canadian Schools*. Final report. Toronto, ON: Egale Canada Human Rights Trust.

Toomey, R. B., Ryan, C., Diaz, R. M., Card, N. A., and Russell, S. T. (2010). Gender-nonconforming lesbian, gay, bisexual, and transgender youth: School victimization and young adult psychosocial adjustment. *Developmental Psychology*, 46(6), 1580–1589. http://doi.org/10.1037/a0020705.

Trans Murdering Monitoring Project (n.d.) Available online: https:// transrespect.org/en/research/trans-murder-monitoring/a0020705.

Travers, R., Bauer, G., Pyne, J., Bradley, K., Gale, L., and Papadimitriou, M. (2012). *Impacts of Strong Parental Support for Trans Youth. TransPULSE*

*Project*. Available online: http://transpulseproject.ca/wp-content/
uploads/2012/10/Impacts-of-Strong-Parental-Support-for-Trans-Youth-
vFINAL.pdf.

van Anders, S., Schudson, Z., Abed, E., Beischel, W., Dibble, E., Gunther,
O., Kutchoko, V., and Silver, E. (2017). Biological sex, gender, and public
policy. *Importance of Biobehavioral Research to Policy*, 4(2), 194–201.

Veale J., Saewyc E., Frohard-Dourlent H., Dobson S., Clark B. and the
Canadian Trans Youth Health Survey Research Group. (2015). *Being Safe,
Being Me: Results of the Canadian Trans Youth Health Survey*. Vancouver,
BC: Stigma and Resilience Among Vulnerable Youth Centre, School of
Nursing, University of British Columbia.

Voss, B. (2018). Cate Blanchett will "Fight to the Death" for Straight Actors to
Play Gay. *Logo: New Now Next*. Available online: www.newnownext.com/
cate-blanchett-fight-to-death-straight-actors-lgbtq-characters/10/2018/.

Wells, K., Roberts, G., and Allan, C. (2012). *Supporting Transgender and
Transsexual Students in K-12 Schools: A Guide for Educators*. Ottawa, ON.

Wells, K., Frohard-Dourlent H., Saewyc E., Ferguson, M., Veale J., and the
Canadian Trans Youth Health Survey Research Group. (2017). *Being Safe,
Being Me in Alberta: Results of the Canadian Trans Youth Health Survey*.
Vancouver, BC: Stigma and Resilience Among Vulnerable Youth Centre,
School of Nursing, University of British Columbia.

Wilchins, R. (2012). Transgender dinosaurs and the rise of the
genderqueers. *Advocate*. Available online: www.advocate.com/
commentary/riki-wilchins/2012/12/06/transgender-dinosaurs-and-rise-
genderqueers?pg=1#article-content.

Winter S, Diamond M, Green J, et al. "Transgender people: health at the
margins of society." *The Lancet*. Published online June 17, 2016. http://
dx.doi.org/10.1016/S0140-6736(16)000683-8.

# Index

Notes: Page numbers in *italics* refer to Figures, and in **bold** refer to definitions and glossary terms. Endnotes are denoted by n. (e.g. 110 n.5)